Bible Promises
to Treasure
for Graduates

Bible Promises
to Treasure
for Graduates

Inspiring

words

for every

occasion

BROADMAN
& HOLMAN
PUBLISHERS

Nashville, Tennessee

Bible Promises to Treasure for Graduates
© 1998 Broadman & Holman Publishers,
Nashville, Tennessee
All rights reserved
Printed in Belgium

ISBN# 1–55819–714–1
Dewey Decimal Classification: 306.87
Subject Heading: GRADUATES
Library of Congress Card Catalog Number: 97–13400

All Scripture passages are from the Authorized King James Version.

******

A note on the sources of quotations. When possible I have supplied at least the book name from which contemporary quotes have come. Yet even this is often impossible, since many came from my "journal of jottings" over many years. Also, if a quote is from a person who lived longer than fifty or so years ago, I've made no attempt to cite the source. Such quotations are usually available in any standard book of quotes.

******

Library of Congress Cataloging-in-Publication Data
Bible promises to treasure for graduates / compiled by Gary Wilde.
    p. cm.
    ISBN 1–55819–714–1
    1. Youth—Religious life—Quotations. 2. Christian life—Quotations, maxims, etc.
    I. Wilde, Gary.
BV4531.2.P76   1998
242'.63—dc21

                                                    97–13400
                                                    CIP

1 2 3 4 5 6   02 01 00 99 98

Contents

Introduction

v

Introduction

I remember as a child singing often at church: "Standing on the Promises of God." Or maybe it was mostly the adults who were singing; but I was standing next to them—my parents and all the others. I recall those faithful people joyfully reciting words they must surely have known by heart . . .

**When the howling storms
of doubt and fear assail,
By the living Word of God I shall prevail,
Standing on the promises of God.**

For years Downey Church, in sunny central Florida, had preached and taught the promises of God and believed in His goodness. From the beginning—when the church building was a

1

small tin-roofed, A-frame at the east end of a dirt road on the outskirts of Orlando—people would gather to stand on the immutable promises. Under the shiny tin roof, standing on the sandy-wooden floorboards, they melded their voices to the tunes of the upright piano and recalled God's goodness. Today, as the church there grows and thrives—now there is also a school and gymnasium—I can only attribute its vibrant life to a love of God's promises and the recognition that without the pledges that flow from the mouth of God, there is no church, no music, and no reason for either.

The promises of God have always been the bedrock of Christian faith; for without God's sacred covenants with us, we cannot survive. In times of joy or heartache, in all our ups and downs, we keep coming back to that source of our life: the motivation for all our doing and the reason for our existence. It is the message of God's mighty assurances: this life is not all there is, He will always be with us while we are here, and He will take us to be with Him someday. Yes, we do have priceless promises to keep close to our hearts!

My hope for you as you delve into this scriptural treasure chest is that you will grow deeper in love with the One who has spoken as no other ever could. With so many influences bombarding our minds each moment of the day, what could be better than to set aside a few moments of quiet to hear the still, small voice that constantly invites us into warm fellowship? We'll be richly rewarded if we truly listen to what that voice is saying. His words convey blessing and guidance, wisdom and warning, life for now and life everlasting. What incomparable grace!

Gary Wilde
Colorado Springs, 1997

One

How Can I Hold on to God's Values?

For so long your parents, teachers, and others told you how to live your life. Now it's time for you to decide. Launching out on your own means greater freedom—and increased responsibility. What kinds of values will motivate your daily decisions and your plans for the future?

Choose Biblical Values for Your Life

I conceive that the great part of the miseries of mankind are brought upon them by false estimates they have made of the value of things.

—*Benjamin Franklin*

Love not the world, neither the things that are in the world. If any man love the world, the love of the Father is not in him.

For all that is in the world, the lust of the flesh, and the lust of the eyes, and the pride of life, is not of the Father, but is of the world.

And the world passeth away, and the lust thereof: but he that doeth the will of God abideth for ever.

—*1 John 2:15–17*

And be not conformed to this world: but be ye transformed by the renewing of your mind, that ye may prove what is that good, and acceptable, and perfect, will of God.

—*Romans 12:2*

Wherefore gird up the loins of your mind, be sober, and hope to the end for the grace that is to be brought unto you at the revelation of Jesus Christ.

—1 Peter 1:13

If ye be reproached for the name of Christ, happy are ye; for the spirit of glory and of God resteth upon you: on their part he is evil spoken of, but on your part he is glorified.

But let none of you suffer as a murderer, or as a thief, or as an evildoer, or as a busybody in other men's matters.

—1 Peter 4:14–15

If the world hate you, ye know that it hated me before it hated you.

If ye were of the world, the world would love his own: but because ye are not of the world, but I have chosen you out of the world, therefore the world hateth you.

—John 15:18–19

Find Your Purpose in the Lord

Lack of something to feel important about is almost the greatest tragedy one may have.

—*Arthur E. Morgan*

I said in mine heart concerning the estate of the sons of men, that God might manifest them, and that they might see that they themselves are beasts.

For that which befalleth the sons of men befalleth beasts; even one thing befalleth them: as the one dieth, so dieth the other; yea, they have all one breath; so that a man hath no preeminence above a beast: for all is vanity.

All go unto one place; all are of the dust, and all turn to dust again.

—*Ecclesiastes 3:18–20*

Let us hear the conclusion of the whole matter: Fear God, and keep his commandments: for this is the whole duty of man.

For God shall bring every work into judgment, with every secret thing, whether it be good, or whether it be evil.

—Ecclesiastes 12:13–14

Maintain the Right Priorities

Teach us that wealth is not elegance, that profusion is not magnificence, that splendor is not beauty.

—Benjamin Disraeli

Whatsoever things are true, whatsoever things are honest, whatsoever things are just, whatsoever things are pure, whatsoever things are lovely, whatsoever things are of good report; if there be any virtue, and if there be any praise, think on these things.

—Philippians 4:8

Therefore we ought to give the more earnest heed to the things which we have heard, lest at any time we should let them slip.

For if the word spoken by angels was stedfast, and every transgression and disobedience received a just recompence of reward;

How shall we escape, if we neglect so great salvation?

—Hebrews 2:1–3a

Wherefore seeing we also are compassed about with so great a cloud of witnesses, let us lay aside every weight, and the sin which doth so easily beset us, and let us run with patience the race that is set before us,

Looking unto Jesus the author and finisher of our faith; who for the joy that was set before him endured the cross, despising the shame, and is set down at the right hand of the throne of God.

—Hebrews 12:1–2

Obey God in Everything

There are two kinds of [persons] who never amount to much: those who cannot do what they are told, and those who can do nothing else.
—*Cyrus H. Curtis*

Whether therefore ye eat, or drink, or whatsoever ye do, do all to the glory of God.
—*1 Corinthians 10:31*

Hereby we do know that we know him, if we keep his commandments.
—*1 John 2:3*

Whosoever believeth that Jesus is the Christ is born of God: and every one that loveth him that begat loveth him also that is begotten of him.

By this we know that we love the children of God, when we love God, and keep his commandments.

For this is the love of God, that we keep his commandments: and his commandments are not grievous.
—*1 John 5:1–3*

Thou shalt love the LORD thy God with all thine heart, and with all thy soul, and with all thy might.

—*Deuteronomy 6:5*

Let the words of my mouth, and the meditation of my heart, be acceptable in thy sight, O LORD, my strength, and my redeemer.

—*Psalm 19:14*

Blessed are the undefiled in the way, who walk in the law of the LORD.

Blessed are they that keep his testimonies, and that seek him with the whole heart.

They also do no iniquity: they walk in his ways.

Thou hast commanded us to keep thy precepts diligently.

O that my ways were directed to keep thy statutes!

—*Psalm 119:1–5*

No man can serve two masters: for either he will hate the one, and love the other; or else he will hold to the one, and despise the other. Ye cannot serve God and mammon.

—*Matthew 6:24*

And [the authorities] called them, and commanded them not to speak at all nor teach in the name of Jesus.

But Peter and John answered and said unto them, Whether it be right in the sight of God to hearken unto you more than unto God, judge ye.

For we cannot but speak the things which we have seen and heard.

—*Acts 4:18–20*

Trust God for What You Need

How calmly may we commit ourselves to the hands of Him who bears up the world.

—Jean Paul Richter

Trust in the LORD with all thine heart; and lean not unto thine own understanding.

In all thy ways acknowledge him, and he shall direct thy paths.

—Proverbs 3:5–6

For what if some did not believe? shall their unbelief make the faith of God without effect?

God forbid: yea, let God be true, but every man a liar.

—Romans 3:3–4a

God made promise to Abraham, . . . Saying, Surely blessing I will bless thee, and multiplying I will multiply thee.

And so, after he had patiently endured, he obtained the promise.

For men verily swear by the greater: and an oath for confirmation is to them an end of all strife.

Wherein God, willing more abundantly to show unto the heirs of promise the immutability of his counsel, confirmed it by an oath:

That by two immutable things, in which it was impossible for God to lie, we might have a strong consolation, who have fled for refuge to lay hold upon the hope set before us:

Which hope we have as an anchor of the soul, both sure and stedfast, and which entereth into that within the veil.

—*Hebrews 6:13–19*

If thou wilt diligently hearken to the voice of the LORD thy God, and wilt do that which is right in his sight, and wilt give ear to his commandments, and keep all his statutes, I will put none of these diseases upon thee, which I have brought upon the Egyptians: for I am the LORD that healeth thee.

—*Exodus 15:26*

For verily I say unto you, That whosoever shall say unto this mountain, Be thou removed, and be thou cast into the sea; and shall not doubt in his heart, but shall believe that those things which he saith shall come to pass; he shall have whatsoever he saith.

—*Mark 11:23*

Let us hold fast the profession of our faith without wavering; (for he is faithful that promised;). . . .

Cast not away therefore your confidence, which hath great recompence of reward.

For ye have need of patience, that, after ye have done the will of God, ye might receive the promise.

For yet a little while, and he that shall come will come, and will not tarry.

—*Hebrews 10:23, 35–37*

Whereby are given unto us exceeding great and precious promises: that by these ye might be partakers of the divine nature, having escaped the corruption that is in the world through lust.

And beside this, giving all diligence, add to your faith virtue; and to virtue knowledge;

And to knowledge temperance; and to temperance patience; and to patience godliness;

And to godliness brotherly kindness; and to brotherly kindness charity.

For if these things be in you, and abound, they make you that ye shall neither be barren nor unfruitful in the knowledge of our Lord Jesus Christ.

—*2 Peter 1:4–8*

And this is the confidence that we have in him, that, if we ask any thing according to his will, he heareth us:

And if we know that he hear us, whatsoever we ask, we know that we have the petitions that we desired of him.

—*1 John 5:14–15*

Keep Growing in Faith

It's not dying for faith that's so hard, it's living up to it.

—*William Makepeace Thackeray*

Then saith he to Thomas, reach hither thy finger, and behold my hands; and reach hither thy hand, and thrust it into my side: and be not faithless, but believing.

And Thomas answered and said unto him, My Lord and my God.

Jesus saith unto him, Thomas, because thou hast seen me, thou hast believed: blessed are they that have not seen, and yet have believed.

And many other signs truly did Jesus in the presence of his disciples, which are not written in this book:

But these are written, that ye might believe that Jesus is the Christ, the Son of God; and that believing ye might have life through his name.

—John 20:27–31

For I know that my redeemer liveth, and that he shall stand at the latter day upon the earth

And though after my skin worms destroy this body, yet in my flesh shall I see God:

Whom I shall see for myself, and mine eyes shall behold, and not another; though my reins be consumed within me.

—Job 19:25–27

Although the fig tree shall not blossom, neither shall fruit be in the vines; the labour of the olive shall fail, and the fields shall yield no meat; the flock shall be cut off from the fold, and there shall be no herd in the stalls:

Yet I will rejoice in the LORD, I will joy in the God of my salvation.

The LORD God is my strength, and he will make my feet like hinds' feet, and he will make me to walk upon mine high places. To the chief singer on my stringed instruments.

—*Habakkuk 3:17–19*

Jesus, walking by the sea of Galilee, saw two brethren, Simon called Peter, and Andrew his brother, casting a net into the sea: for they were fishers.

And he saith unto them, Follow me, and I will make you fishers of men.

And they straightway left their nets, and followed him.

And going on from thence, he saw other two brethren, James the son of Zebedee, and John his brother, in a ship with Zebedee their father, mending their nets; and he called them.

And they immediately left the ship and their father, and followed him.

—*Matthew 4:18–22*

Reach Out with Godly Compassion

The value of compassion cannot be over-emphasized. Anyone can criticize. It takes a true believer to be compassionate. No greater burden can be borne by an individual than to know no one cares or understands.

—Arthur H. Stainback

And, behold, a certain lawyer stood up, and tempted him, saying, Master, what shall I do to inherit eternal life?

He said unto him, What is written in the law? how readest thou?

And he answering said, Thou shalt love the Lord thy God with all thy heart, and with all thy soul, and with all thy strength, and with all thy mind; and thy neighbour as thyself.

And he said unto him, Thou hast answered right: this do, and thou shalt live.

But he, willing to justify himself, said unto Jesus, And who is my neighbour?

And Jesus answering said, A certain man went down from Jerusalem to Jericho, and fell among thieves, which stripped him of his raiment, and wounded him, and departed, leaving him half dead.

And by chance there came down a certain priest that way: and when he saw him, he passed by on the other side.

And likewise a Levite, when he was at the place, came and looked on him, and passed by on the other side.

But a certain Samaritan, as he journeyed, came where he was: and when he saw him, he had compassion on him,

And went to him, and bound up his wounds, pouring in oil and wine, and set him on his own beast, and brought him to an inn, and took care of him.

And on the morrow when he departed, he took out two pence, and gave them to the host, and said unto him, Take care of him; and whatsoever thou spendest more, when I come again, I will repay thee.

Which now of these three, thinkest thou, was neighbour unto him that fell among the thieves?

And he said, He that shewed mercy on him. Then said Jesus unto him, Go, and do thou likewise.

—Luke 10:25–37

When [the daughter of Pharaoh] had opened [the ark], she saw the child: and, behold, the babe wept. And she had compassion on him, and said, This is one of the Hebrews' children.

Then said his sister to Pharaoh's daughter, Shall I go and call to thee a nurse of the Hebrew women, that she may nurse the child for thee?

And Pharaoh's daughter said to her, Go. And the maid went and called the child's mother.

And Pharaoh's daughter said unto her, Take this child away, and nurse it for me, and I will give thee thy wages. And the woman took the child, and nursed it.

And the child grew, and she brought him unto Pharaoh's daughter, and he became her son. And she called his name Moses: and she said, Because I drew him out of the water.

—Exodus 2:6–10

Of some have compassion, making a difference:

And others save with fear, pulling them out of the fire; hating even the garment spotted by the flesh.

—Jude 22–23

Where Can I Find God's Wisdom?

Everyone has a piece of advice for us when we're young and seeking direction in life. But often we receive so-called wisdom that won't hold up for long amidst the real challenges of daily living. That is not the case with God's "advice," however. His wisdom is immediately applicable and eternally beneficial—if only we will seek it out by listening closely to the One who taught it best.

It's Wise to Follow Jesus When He Calls

The voice that we hear over our shoulders never says, "First be sure that your motives are pure and selfless and then follow me." If it did, then we could none of us follow. So when later the voice says, "Take up your cross and follow me," at least part of what is meant by "cross" is our realization that we are seldom any less than nine parts fake. Yet our feet can insist on answering him anyway, and on we go, step after step, mile after mile. How far? How far?

—Frederick Buechner [1]

Then he called his twelve disciples together, and gave them power and authority over all devils, and to cure diseases.

And he sent them to preach the kingdom of God, and to heal the sick.

And he said unto them, Take nothing for your journey, neither staves, nor scrip, neither bread, neither money; neither have two coats apiece.

And whatsoever house ye enter into, there abide, and thence depart.

And whosoever will not receive you, when ye go out of that city, shake off the very dust from your feet for a testimony against them.

—*Luke 9:1–5*

[Jesus] said to them all, If any man will come after me, let him deny himself, and take up his cross daily, and follow me.

For whosoever will save his life shall lose it: but whosoever will lose his life for my sake, the same shall save it.

For what is a man advantaged, if he gain the whole world, and lose himself, or be cast away?

—*Luke 9:23–25*

Jesus answered them, saying, The hour is come, that the Son of man should be glorified.

Verily, verily, I say unto you, Except a corn of wheat fall into the ground and die, it abideth alone: but if it die, it bringeth forth much fruit.

He that loveth his life shall lose it; and he that hateth his life in this world shall keep it unto life eternal.

25

If any man serve me, let him follow me; and where I am, there shall also my servant be: if any man serve me, him will my Father honour.

—John 12:23–26

Little children, yet a little while I am with you. Ye shall seek me: and as I said unto the Jews, Whither I go, ye cannot come, so now I say to you.

A new commandment I give unto you, That ye love one another; as I have loved you, that ye also love one another.

By this shall all men know that ye are my disciples, if ye have love one to another.

Simon Peter said unto him, Lord, whither goest thou? Jesus answered him, Whither I go, thou canst not follow me now; but thou shalt follow me afterwards.

—John 13:33–36

He Taught in Parables . . .

You cannot teach a man anything; you can only help him find it within himself.

—Galileo

Son of man, put forth a riddle, and speak a parable unto the house of Israel.

—Ezekiel 17:2

I will open my mouth in a parable: I will utter dark sayings of old.

—Psalm 78:2

[Jesus] said, Unto you it is given to know the mysteries of the kingdom of God: but to others in parables; that seeing they might not see, and hearing they might not understand.

—Luke 8:10

So Learn from Your Master Teacher . . .

He who adds not to his learning diminishes it.[2]
—The Talmud

About Wisdom and Foolishness

Therefore whosoever heareth these sayings of mine, and doeth them, I will liken him unto a wise man, which built his house upon a rock:

And the rain descended, and the floods came, and the winds blew, and beat upon that house; and it fell not: for it was founded upon a rock.

And every one that heareth these sayings of mine, and doeth them not, shall be likened unto a foolish man, which built his house upon the sand:

And the rain descended, and the floods came, and the winds blew, and beat upon that house; and it fell: and great was the fall of it.

—*Matthew 7:24–27*

🍃 *About Forgiveness*

There was a certain creditor which had two debtors: the one owed five hundred pence, and the other fifty.

And when they had nothing to pay, he frankly forgave them both. Tell me therefore, which of them will love him most?

Simon answered and said, I suppose that he, to whom he forgave most. And he said unto him, Thou hast rightly judged.

And he turned to the woman, and said unto Simon, Seest thou this woman? I entered into thine house, thou gavest me no water for my feet: but she hath washed my feet with tears, and wiped them with the hairs of her head.

Thou gavest me no kiss: but this woman since the time I came in hath not ceased to kiss my feet.

My head with oil thou didst not anoint: but this woman hath anointed my feet with ointment.

Wherefore I say unto thee, Her sins, which are many, are forgiven; for she loved much: but to whom little is forgiven, the same loveth little.

—Luke 7:41–47

🖋 About Being Alert

Let your loins be girded about, and your lights burning;

And ye yourselves like unto men that wait for their lord, when he will return from the wedding; that when he cometh and knocketh, they may open unto him immediately.

Blessed are those servants, whom the lord when he cometh shall find watching: verily I say unto you, that he shall gird himself, and make them to sit down to meat, and will come forth and serve them.

And if he shall come in the second watch, or come in the third watch, and find them so, blessed are those servants.

And this know, that if the goodman of the house had known what hour the thief would come, he would have watched, and not have suffered his house to be broken through.

Be ye therefore ready also: for the Son of man cometh at an hour when ye think not.

—*Luke 12:35–40*

About the Right Priorities

[Jesus] spake a parable unto them, saying, The ground of a certain rich man brought forth plentifully:

And he thought within himself, saying, What shall I do, because I have no room where to bestow my fruits?

And he said, This will I do: I will pull down my barns, and build greater; and there will I bestow all my fruits and my goods.

And I will say to my soul, Soul, thou hast much goods laid up for many years; take thine ease, eat, drink, and be merry.

But God said unto him, Thou fool, this night thy soul shall be required of thee: then whose shall those things be, which thou hast provided?

So is he that layeth up treasure for himself, and is not rich toward God.

—*Luke 12:16–21*

🍃 About Showing Mercy

Therefore is the kingdom of heaven likened unto a certain king, which would take account of his servants.

And when he had begun to reckon, one was brought unto him, which owed him ten thousand talents.

But forasmuch as he had not to pay, his lord commanded him to be sold, and his wife, and children, and all that he had, and payment to be made.

The servant therefore fell down, and worshipped him, saying, Lord, have patience with me, and I will pay thee all.

Then the lord of that servant was moved with compassion, and loosed him, and forgave him the debt.

But the same servant went out, and found one of his fellowservants, which owed him an hundred pence: and he laid hands on him, and took him by the throat, saying, Pay me that thou owest.

And his fellowservant fell down at his feet, and besought him, saying, Have patience with me, and I will pay thee all.

And he would not: but went and cast him into prison, till he should pay the debt.

So when his fellowservants saw what was done, they were very sorry, and came and told unto their lord all that was done.

Then his lord, after that he had called him, said unto him, O thou wicked servant, I forgave thee all that debt, because thou desiredst me:

Shouldest not thou also have had compassion on thy fellowservant, even as I had pity on thee?

And his lord was wroth, and delivered him to the tormentors, till he should pay all that was due unto him.

So likewise shall my heavenly Father do also unto you, if ye from your hearts forgive not every one his brother their trespasses.

—*Matthew 18:23–35*

 ## *About Persistence*

And he said unto them, Which of you shall have a friend, and shall go unto him at midnight, and say unto him, Friend, lend me three loaves;

For a friend of mine in his journey is come to me, and I have nothing to set before him?

And he from within shall answer and say, Trouble me not: the door is now shut, and my children are with me in bed; I cannot rise and give thee.

I say unto you, Though he will not rise and give him, because he is his friend, yet because of his importunity he will rise and give him as many as he needeth.

—*Luke 11:5–8*

About the Power of the Word

[Jesus] began again to teach by the sea side: and there was gathered unto him a great multitude, so that he entered into a ship, and sat in the sea; and the whole multitude was by the sea on the land.

And he taught them many things by parables, and said unto them in his doctrine,

Hearken; Behold, there went out a sower to sow:

And it came to pass, as he sowed, some fell by the way side, and the fowls of the air came and devoured it up.

And some fell on stony ground, where it had not much earth; and immediately it sprang up, because it had no depth of earth:

But when the sun was up, it was scorched; and because it had no root, it withered away.

And some fell among thorns, and the thorns grew up, and choked it, and it yielded no fruit.

And other fell on good ground, and did yield fruit that sprang up and increased; and brought forth, some thirty, and some sixty, and some an hundred.

And he said unto them, He that hath ears to hear, let him hear.

And when he was alone, they that were about him with the twelve asked of him the parable.

And he said unto them, Unto you it is given to know the mystery of the kingdom of God: but unto them that are without, all these things are done in parables:

That seeing they may see, and not perceive; and hearing they may hear, and not understand; lest at any time they should be converted, and their sins should be forgiven them.

And he said unto them, Know ye not this parable? and how then will ye know all parables?

The sower soweth the word.

And these are they by the way side, where the word is sown; but when they have heard, Satan cometh immediately, and taketh away the word that was sown in their hearts.

And these are they likewise which are sown on stony ground; who, when they have heard the word, immediately receive it with gladness;

And have no root in themselves, and so endure but for a time: afterward, when affliction or persecution ariseth for the word's sake, immediately they are offended.

And these are they which are sown among thorns; such as hear the word,

And the cares of this world, and the deceitfulness of riches, and the lusts of other things entering in, choke the word, and it becometh unfruitful.

And these are they which are sown on good ground; such as hear the word, and receive it, and bring forth fruit, some thirty-fold, some sixty, and some an hundred.

—*Mark 4:1–20*

About Responding to God's Grace

And when one of them that sat at meat with [Jesus] heard these things, he said unto him, Blessed is he that shall eat bread in the kingdom of God.

Then said he unto him, A certain man made a great supper, and bade many:

And sent his servant at supper time to say to them that were bidden, Come; for all things are now ready.

And they all with one consent began to make excuse. The first said unto him, I have bought a piece of ground, and I must needs go and see it: I pray thee have me excused.

And another said, I have bought five yoke of oxen, and I go to prove them: I pray thee have me excused.

And another said, I have married a wife, and therefore I cannot come.

So that servant came, and shewed his lord these things. Then the master of the house being angry said to his servant, Go out quickly into the streets and lanes of the city, and bring in hither the poor, and the maimed, and the halt, and the blind.

And the servant said, Lord, it is done as thou hast commanded, and yet there is room.

And the lord said unto the servant, Go out into the highways and hedges, and compel them to come in, that my house may be filled.

For I say unto you, That none of those men which were bidden shall taste of my supper.

—Luke 14:15–24

About Prudence in Spiritual Matters

[Jesus] also unto his disciples, There was a certain rich man, which had a steward; and the same was accused unto him that he had wasted his goods.

And he called him, and said unto him, How is it that I hear this of thee? give an account of thy stewardship; for thou mayest be no longer steward.

Then the steward said within himself, What shall I do? for my lord taketh away from me the stewardship: I cannot dig; to beg I am ashamed.

I am resolved what to do, that, when I am put out of the stewardship, they may receive me into their houses.

So he called every one of his lord's debtors unto him, and said unto the first, How much owest thou unto my lord?

And he said, An hundred measures of oil. And he said unto him, Take thy bill, and sit down quickly, and write fifty.

Then said he to another, And how much owest thou? And he said, An hundred measures of wheat. And he said unto him, Take thy bill, and write fourscore.

And the lord commended the unjust steward, because he had done wisely: for the children of this world are in their generation wiser than the children of light.

And I say unto you, Make to yourselves friends of the mammon of unrighteousness; that, when ye fail, they may receive you into everlasting habitations.

—*Luke 16:1–9*

About Urgently Entreating God

[Jesus] spake a parable unto them to this end, that men ought always to pray, and not to faint;

Saying, There was in a city a judge, which feared not God, neither regarded man:

And there was a widow in that city; and she came unto him, saying, Avenge me of mine adversary.

And he would not for a while: but afterward he said within himself, Though I fear not God, nor regard man;

Yet because this widow troubleth me, I will avenge her, lest by her continual coming she weary me.

And the Lord said, Hear what the unjust judge saith.

And shall not God avenge his own elect, which cry day and night unto him, though he bear long with them?

I tell you that he will avenge them speedily. Nevertheless when the Son of man cometh, shall he find faith on the earth?

—Luke 18:1–8

🌱 About Pride and Humility

[Jesus] spake this parable unto certain which trusted in themselves that they were righteous, and despised others:

Two men went up into the temple to pray; the one a Pharisee, and the other a publican.

The Pharisee stood and prayed thus with himself, God, I thank thee, that I am not as other men are, extortioners, unjust, adulterers, or even as this publican.

I fast twice in the week, I give tithes of all that I possess.

And the publican, standing afar off, would not lift up so much as his eyes unto heaven, but smote upon his breast, saying, God be merciful to me a sinner.

I tell you, this man went down to his house justified rather than the other: for every one that exalteth himself shall be abased; and he that humbleth himself shall be exalted.

—*Luke 18:9–14*

About Working in the Kingdom

For the kingdom of heaven is like unto a man that is an householder, which went out early in the morning to hire labourers into his vineyard.

And when he had agreed with the labourers for a penny a day, he sent them into his vineyard.

And he went out about the third hour, and saw others standing idle in the marketplace,

And said unto them; Go ye also into the vineyard, and whatsoever is right I will give you. And they went their way.

Again he went out about the sixth and ninth hour, and did likewise.

And about the eleventh hour he went out, and found others standing idle, and saith unto them, Why stand ye here all the day idle?

They say unto him, Because no man hath hired us. He saith unto them, Go ye also into the vineyard; and whatsoever is right, that shall ye receive.

So when even was come, the lord of the vineyard saith unto his steward, Call the labourers, and give them their hire, beginning from the last unto the first.

And when they came that were hired about the eleventh hour, they received every man a penny.

But when the first came, they supposed that they should have received more; and they likewise received every man a penny.

And when they had received it, they murmured against the goodman of the house,

Saying, These last have wrought but one hour, and thou hast made them equal unto us, which have borne the burden and heat of the day.

But he answered one of them, and said, Friend, I do thee no wrong: didst not thou agree with me for a penny?

Take that thine is, and go thy way: I will give unto this last, even as unto thee.

Is it not lawful for me to do what I will with mine own? Is thine eye evil, because I am good?

So the last shall be first, and the first last: for many be called, but few chosen.

—*Matthew 20:1–16*

About Being Ready for His Coming

For the kingdom of heaven is as a man travelling into a far country, who called his own servants, and delivered unto them his goods.

And unto one he gave five talents, to another two, and to another one; to every man according to his several ability; and straightway took his journey.

Then he that had received the five talents went and traded with the same, and made them other five talents.

And likewise he that had received two, he also gained other two.

But he that had received one went and digged in the earth, and hid his lord's money.

After a long time the lord of those servants cometh, and reckoneth with them.

And so he that had received five talents came and brought other five talents, saying, Lord, thou deliveredst unto me five talents: behold, I have gained beside them five talents more.

His lord said unto him, Well done, thou good and faithful servant: thou hast been faithful over a few things, I will make thee ruler over many things: enter thou into the joy of thy lord.

He also that had received two talents came and said, Lord, thou deliveredst unto me two talents: behold, I have gained two other talents beside them.

His lord said unto him, Well done, good and faithful servant; thou hast been faithful over a few things, I will make thee ruler over many things: enter thou into the joy of thy lord.

Then he which had received the one talent came and said, Lord, I knew thee that thou art an hard man, reaping where thou hast not sown, and gathering where thou hast not strawed:

And I was afraid, and went and hid thy talent in the earth: lo, there thou hast that is thine.

His lord answered and said unto him, Thou wicked and slothful servant, thou knewest that I reap where I sowed not, and gather where I have not strawed:

Thou oughtest therefore to have put my money to the exchangers, and then at my coming I should have received mine own with usury.

Take therefore the talent from him, and give it unto him which hath ten talents.

For unto every one that hath shall be given, and he shall have abundance: but from him that hath not shall be taken away even that which he hath.

And cast ye the unprofitable servant into outer darkness: there shall be weeping and gnashing of teeth.

—Matthew 25:14–30

Keep On Learning, Throughout Your Life

The wisest mind has something yet to learn.
—George Santayana

I am thy servant; give me understanding, that I may know thy testimonies.

—Psalm 119:125

The fear of the LORD is the beginning of wisdom: a good understanding have all they that do his commandments: his praise endureth for ever.

—Psalm 111:10

If any of you lack wisdom, let him ask of God, that giveth to all men liberally, and upbraideth not; and it shall be given him.

But let him ask in faith, nothing wavering. For he that wavereth is like a wave of the sea driven with the wind and tossed.

For let not that man think that he shall receive any thing of the Lord.

A double minded man is unstable in all his ways.

—*James 1:5–8*

And when they bring you unto the synagogues, and unto magistrates, and powers, take ye no thought how or what thing ye shall answer, or what ye shall say:

For the Holy Ghost shall teach you in the same hour what ye ought to say.

—*Luke 12:11–12*

For I will give you a mouth and wisdom, which all your adversaries shall not be able to gainsay nor resist.

—*Luke 21:15*

Consider what I say; and the Lord give thee understanding in all things.

—*2 Timothy 2:7*

Seek Divine Guidance for Your Future

Scripture tells us that we must become like little children, and that the teaching we need is right here if we have eyes to see and ears to hear. It tells us that we live and move and have our being in a divine One who is already at home is us, ready to guide us where we need to go. It tells us that Holy Wisdom cries in the streets for us, promising that in self-abandonment we will never be abandoned. It assures us that we will find what we seek, that we shall know the truth, and that it will make us free.

—*Gerald May* [3]

Man's goings are of the LORD; how can a man then understand his own way?

—*Proverbs 20:24*

Thus saith the LORD, thy Redeemer, the Holy One of Israel; I am the LORD thy God which teacheth thee to profit, which leadeth thee by the way that thou shouldest go.

O that thou hadst hearkened to my commandments! then had thy peace been as a river, and thy righteousness as the waves of the sea.

—*Isaiah 48:17–18*

They shall not hunger nor thirst; neither shall the heat nor sun smite them: for he that hath mercy on them shall lead them, even by the springs of water shall he guide them.

And I will make all my mountains a way, and my highways shall be exalted.

—*Isaiah 49:10–11*

Three

Do I Have Any Role Models to Follow?

Have you noticed the people held up to us as "heroes" today? The athletes, the music stars, the talk-show celebrities—all have something to say about what it means to be a success. And their influence is pervasive, though subtle.

Yet what kind of influence is it? And are there any other heroes available? In the Bible, for instance?

Realize the Power of Others' Influence on You . . .

The least movement is of importance to all nature. The entire ocean is affected by a pebble.

—Blaise Pascal

I write not these things to shame you, but as my beloved sons I warn you.

For though ye have ten thousand instructors in Christ, yet have ye not many fathers: for in Christ Jesus I have begotten you through the gospel.

Wherefore I beseech you, be ye followers of me.

—1 Corinthians 4:14–16

Beloved, follow not that which is evil, but that which is good. He that doeth good is of God: but he that doeth evil hath not seen God.

—3 John 11

Take, my brethren, the prophets, who have spoken in the name of the Lord, for an example of suffering affliction, and of patience.

—*James 5:10*

✎ *For Good*

And all the people that were in the gate, and the elders, said, We are witnesses. The LORD make the woman that is come into thine house like Rachel and like Leah, which two did build the house of Israel: and do thou worthily in Ephratah, and be famous in Bethlehem.

—*Ruth 4:11*

Children's children are the crown of old men; and the glory of children are their fathers.

—*Proverbs 17:6*

As ye know how we exhorted and comforted and charged every one of you, as a father doth his children,

That ye would walk worthy of God, who hath called you unto his kingdom and glory.

—*1 Thessalonians 2:11–12*

When I call to remembrance the unfeigned faith that is in thee, which dwelt first in thy grandmother Lois, and thy mother Eunice; and I am persuaded that in thee also.

—*2 Timothy 1:5*

I rejoiced greatly that I found of thy children walking in truth, as we have received a commandment from the Father.

—*2 John 4*

For Bad

Thou shalt not follow a multitude to do evil; neither shalt thou speak in a cause to decline after many to wrest judgment.

—*Exodus 23:2*

As did their fathers, so do they unto this day.

—*2 Kings 17:41b*

And there are gathered unto him vain men, the children of Belial, and have strengthened themselves against Rehoboam the son of Solomon, when Rehoboam was young and tenderhearted, and could not withstand them.

—*2 Chronicles 13:7*

Make no friendship with an angry man;
and with a furious man thou shalt not go.

—Proverbs 22:24

That pant after the dust of the earth on the
head of the poor, and turn aside the way of the
meek: and a man and his father will go in unto
the same maid, to profane my holy name.

—Amos 2:7

But whoso shall offend one of these little
ones which believe in me, it were better for
him that a millstone were hanged about his
neck, and that he were drowned in the depth
of the sea.

—Matthew 18:6

So Emulate Exemplary Women . . .

Blessed is the influence of one true, loving human soul on another.

—*Marian Evans Cross*

Moses' Mother

And there went a man of the house of Levi, and took to wife a daughter of Levi.

And the woman conceived, and bare a son: and when she saw him that he was a goodly child, she hid him three months.

And when she could not longer hide him, she took for him an ark of bulrushes, and daubed it with slime and with pitch, and put the child therein; and she laid it in the flags by the river's brink.

And his sister stood afar off, to wit what would be done to him.

And the daughter of Pharaoh came down to wash herself at the river; and her maidens walked along by the river's side; and when she saw the ark among the flags, she sent her maid to fetch it.

And when she had opened it, she saw the child: and, behold, the babe wept. And she had compassion on him, and said, This is one of the Hebrews' children.

Then said his sister to Pharaoh's daughter, Shall I go and call to thee a nurse of the Hebrew women, that she may nurse the child for thee?

And Pharaoh's daughter said to her, Go. And the maid went and called the child's mother.

And Pharaoh's daughter said unto her, Take this child away, and nurse it for me, and I will give thee thy wages. And the woman took the child, and nursed it.

And the child grew, and she brought him unto Pharaoh's daughter, and he became her son. And she called his name Moses: and she said, Because I drew him out of the water.

—*Exodus 2:1–10*

Hannah: A Woman Who Knew How to Pray

[Hannah] was in bitterness of soul, and prayed unto the LORD, and wept sore.

And she vowed a vow, and said, O LORD of hosts, if thou wilt indeed look on the affliction of thine handmaid, and remember me, and not forget thine handmaid, but wilt give unto thine handmaid a man child, then I will give him unto the LORD all the days of his life, and there shall no razor come upon his head.

And it came to pass, as she continued praying before the LORD, that Eli marked her mouth.

Now Hannah, she spake in her heart; only her lips moved, but her voice was not heard: therefore Eli thought she had been drunken.

And Eli said unto her, How long wilt thou be drunken? put away thy wine from thee.

And Hannah answered and said, No, my lord, I am a woman of a sorrowful spirit: I have drunken neither wine nor strong drink, but have poured out my soul before the LORD.

Count not thine handmaid for a daughter of Belial: for out of the abundance of my complaint and grief have I spoken hitherto.

Then Eli answered and said, Go in peace: and the God of Israel grant thee thy petition that thou hast asked of him.

And she said, Let thine handmaid find grace in thy sight. So the woman went her way, and did eat, and her countenance was no more sad.

And they rose up in the morning early, and worshipped before the LORD, and returned, and came to their house to Ramah: and Elkanah knew Hannah his wife; and the LORD remembered her.

Wherefore it came to pass, when the time was come about after Hannah had conceived, that she bare a son, and called his name Samuel, saying, Because I have asked him of the LORD.

And the man Elkanah, and all his house, went up to offer unto the LORD the yearly sacrifice, and his vow.

But Hannah went not up; for she said unto her husband, I will not go up until the child be weaned, and then I will bring him, that he may appear before the LORD, and there abide for ever.

And Elkanah her husband said unto her, Do what seemeth thee good; tarry until thou have weaned him; only the LORD establish his word. So the woman abode, and gave her son suck until she weaned him.

And when she had weaned him, she took him up with her, with three bullocks, and one ephah of flour, and a bottle of wine, and brought him unto the house of the LORD in Shiloh: and the child was young.

And they slew a bullock, and brought the child to Eli.

And she said, Oh my lord, as thy soul liveth, my lord, I am the woman that stood by thee here, praying unto the LORD.

For this child I prayed; and the LORD hath given me my petition which I asked of him:

Therefore also I have lent him to the LORD; as long as he liveth he shall be lent to the LORD. And he worshipped the LORD there.

—1 Samuel 1:10–28

Mary: She Rejoiced in God

In the sixth month the angel Gabriel was sent from God unto a city of Galilee, named Nazareth,

To a virgin espoused to a man whose name was Joseph, of the house of David; and the virgin's name was Mary.

And the angel came in unto her, and said, Hail, thou that art highly favoured, the Lord is with thee: blessed art thou among women.

And when she saw him, she was troubled at his saying, and cast in her mind what manner of salutation this should be.

And the angel said unto her, Fear not, Mary: for thou hast found favour with God.

And, behold, thou shalt conceive in thy womb, and bring forth a son, and shalt call his name JESUS. . . .

And Mary said, My soul doth magnify the Lord,

And my spirit hath rejoiced in God my Saviour.

For he hath regarded the low estate of his handmaiden: for, behold, from henceforth all generations shall call me blessed.

For he that is mighty hath done to me great things; and holy is his name.

And his mercy is on them that fear him from generation to generation.

He hath shewed strength with his arm; he hath scattered the proud in the imagination of their hearts.

He hath put down the mighty from their seats, and exalted them of low degree.

He hath filled the hungry with good things;
and the rich he hath sent empty away.

—*Luke 1:26–31, 46–53*

🔖 *Sarah: Willing to Adjust to a New Life*

God said unto Abraham, As for Sarai thy
wife, thou shalt not call her name Sarai, but
Sarah shall her name be.

And I will bless her, and give thee a son also
of her: yea, I will bless her, and she shall be a
mother of nations; kings of people shall be
of her.

Then Abraham fell upon his face, and
laughed, and said in his heart, Shall a child be
born unto him that is an hundred years old?
and shall Sarah, that is ninety years old, bear?

And Abraham said unto God, O that Ish-
mael might live before thee!

And God said, Sarah thy wife shall bear
thee a son indeed; and thou shalt call his
name Isaac: and I will establish my covenant
with him for an everlasting covenant, and
with his seed after him. . . .

And they said unto him, Where is Sarah thy wife? And he said, Behold, in the tent.

And he said, I will certainly return unto thee according to the time of life; and, lo, Sarah thy wife shall have a son. And Sarah heard it in the tent door, which was behind him.

Now Abraham and Sarah were old and well stricken in age; and it ceased to be with Sarah after the manner of women.

Therefore Sarah laughed within herself, saying, After I am waxed old shall I have pleasure, my lord being old also?

And the LORD said unto Abraham, Wherefore did Sarah laugh, saying, Shall I of a surety bear a child, which am old?

Is any thing too hard for the LORD? At the time appointed I will return unto thee, according to the time of life, and Sarah shall have a son. . . .

And the LORD visited Sarah as he had said, and the LORD did unto Sarah as he had spoken.

For Sarah conceived, and bare Abraham a son in his old age, at the set time of which God had spoken to him.

And Abraham called the name of his son that was born unto him, whom Sarah bare to him, Isaac.

—*Genesis 17:15–19; 18:9–14; 21:1–3*

And Make These Men Your Mentors . . .

Other men are lenses through which we read our own minds.

—*Ralph Waldo Emerson*

He that walketh with wise men shall be wise: but a companion of fools shall be destroyed.

—*Proverbs 13:20*

⚑ A Man of Faith

Now the LORD had said unto Abram, Get thee out of thy country, and from thy kindred, and from thy father's house, unto a land that I will shew thee:

And I will make of thee a great nation, and I will bless thee, and make thy name great; and thou shalt be a blessing:

And I will bless them that bless thee, and curse him that curseth thee: and in thee shall all families of the earth be blessed.

So Abram departed, as the LORD had spoken unto him; and Lot went with him: and Abram was seventy and five years old when he departed out of Haran.

And Abram took Sarai his wife, and Lot his brother's son, and all their substance that they had gathered, and the souls that they had gotten in Haran; and they went forth to go into the land of Canaan; and into the land of Canaan they came.

And Abram passed through the land unto the place of Sichem, unto the plain of Moreh. And the Canaanite was then in the land.

And the LORD appeared unto Abram, and said, Unto thy seed will I give this land: and there builded he an altar unto the LORD, who appeared unto him.

And he removed from thence unto a mountain on the east of Bethel, and pitched his tent, having Bethel on the west, and Hai on the east: and there he builded an altar unto the LORD, and called upon the name of the LORD.

And Abram journeyed, going on still toward the south.

—*Genesis 12:1–9*

A Man of Bold Action

Joshua gathered all the tribes of Israel to Shechem, and called for the elders of Israel, and for their heads, and for their judges, and for their officers; and they presented themselves before God.

And Joshua said unto all the people, Thus saith the LORD God of Israel, Your fathers dwelt on the other side of the flood in old time, even Terah, the father of Abraham, and the father of Nachor: and they served other gods. . . .

Now therefore fear the LORD, and serve him in sincerity and in truth: and put away the gods which your fathers served on the other side of the flood, and in Egypt; and serve ye the LORD.

And if it seem evil unto you to serve the LORD, choose you this day whom ye will serve; whether the gods which your fathers served that were on the other side of the flood, or the gods of the Amorites, in whose land ye dwell: but as for me and my house, we will serve the LORD.

—Joshua 24:1–2, 14–15

A Man Who Could Forgive

Then Joseph could not refrain himself before all them that stood by him; and he cried, Cause every man to go out from me. And there stood no man with him, while Joseph made himself known unto his brethren.

And he wept aloud: and the Egyptians and the house of Pharaoh heard.

And Joseph said unto his brethren, I am Joseph; doth my father yet live? And his brethren could not answer him; for they were troubled at his presence.

And Joseph said unto his brethren, Come near to me, I pray you. And they came near. And he said, I am Joseph your brother, whom ye sold into Egypt.

Now therefore be not grieved, nor angry with yourselves, that ye sold me hither: for God did send me before you to preserve life.

—Genesis 45:1–5

A Man Who Admitted His Sin

The LORD sent Nathan unto David. And he came unto him, and said unto him, There were two men in one city; the one rich, and the other poor.

The rich man had exceeding many flocks and herds:

But the poor man had nothing, save one little ewe lamb, which he had bought and nourished up: and it grew up together with him, and with his children; it did eat of his own meat, and drank of his own cup, and lay in his bosom, and was unto him as a daughter.

And there came a traveller unto the rich man, and he spared to take of his own flock and of his own herd, to dress for the wayfaring man that was come unto him; but took the poor man's lamb, and dressed it for the man that was come to him.

And David's anger was greatly kindled against the man; and he said to Nathan, As the LORD liveth, the man that hath done this thing shall surely die:

And he shall restore the lamb fourfold, because he did this thing, and because he had no pity.

And Nathan said to David, Thou art the man. Thus saith the LORD God of Israel, I anointed thee king over Israel, and I delivered thee out of the hand of Saul;

And I gave thee thy master's house, and thy master's wives into thy bosom, and gave thee the house of Israel and of Judah; and if that had been too little, I would moreover have given unto thee such and such things.

Wherefore hast thou despised the commandment of the LORD, to do evil in his sight? thou hast killed Uriah the Hittite with the sword, and hast taken his wife to be thy wife, and hast slain him with the sword of the children of Ammon.

Now therefore the sword shall never depart from thine house; because thou hast despised me, and hast taken the wife of Uriah the Hittite to be thy wife.

Thus saith the LORD, Behold, I will raise up evil against thee out of thine own house, and I will take thy wives before thine eyes, and give them unto thy neighbour, and he shall lie with thy wives in the sight of this sun.

For thou didst it secretly: but I will do this thing before all Israel, and before the sun.

And David said unto Nathan, I have sinned against the LORD.

—*2 Samuel 12:1–13a*

A Man of Courage

Now when Daniel knew that the writing was signed, he went into his house; and his windows being open in his chamber toward Jerusalem, he kneeled upon his knees three times a day, and prayed, and gave thanks before his God, as he did aforetime.

Then these men assembled, and found Daniel praying and making supplication before his God.

Then they came near, and spake before the king concerning the king's decree; Hast thou not signed a decree, that every man that shall ask a petition of any God or man within thirty days, save of thee, O king, shall be cast into the den of lions? The king answered and said,

The thing is true, according to the law of the Medes and Persians, which altereth not.

Then answered they and said before the king, That Daniel, which is of the children of the captivity of Judah, regardeth not thee, O king, nor the decree that thou hast signed, but maketh his petition three times a day.

Then the king, when he heard these words, was sore displeased with himself, and set his heart on Daniel to deliver him: and he laboured till the going down of the sun to deliver him.

Then these men assembled unto the king, and said unto the king, Know, O king, that the law of the Medes and Persians is, That no decree nor statute which the king establisheth may be changed.

Then the king commanded, and they brought Daniel, and cast him into the den of lions. Now the king spake and said unto Daniel, Thy God whom thou servest continually, he will deliver thee.

And a stone was brought and laid upon the mouth of the den; and the king sealed it with his own signet, and with the signet of his lords; that the purpose might not be changed concerning Daniel.

Then the king went to his palace, and passed the night fasting: neither were instruments of musick brought before him: and his sleep went from him.

Then the king arose very early in the morning, and went in haste unto the den of lions.

And when he came to the den, he cried with a lamentable voice unto Daniel: and the king spake and said to Daniel, O Daniel, servant of the living God, is thy God, whom thou servest continually, able to deliver thee from the lions?

Then said Daniel unto the king, O king, live for ever.

My God hath sent his angel, and hath shut the lions' mouths, that they have not hurt me: forasmuch as before him innocency was found in me; and also before thee, O king, have I done no hurt.

Then was the king exceeding glad for him, and commanded that they should take Daniel up out of the den. So Daniel was taken up out of the den, and no manner of hurt was found upon him, because he believed in his God.

—*Daniel 6:10–23*

A Man Who Witnessed to Christ

The day following Jesus would go forth into Galilee, and findeth Philip, and saith unto him, Follow me.

Now Philip was of Bethsaida, the city of Andrew and Peter.

Philip findeth Nathanael, and saith unto him, We have found him, of whom Moses in the law, and the prophets, did write, Jesus of Nazareth, the son of Joseph.

And Nathanael said unto him, Can there any good thing come out of Nazareth? Philip saith unto him, Come and see.

Jesus saw Nathanael coming to him, and saith of him, Behold an Israelite indeed, in whom is no guile!

Nathanael saith unto him, Whence knowest thou me? Jesus answered and said unto him, Before that Philip called thee, when thou wast under the fig tree, I saw thee.

Nathanael answered and saith unto him, Rabbi, thou art the Son of God; thou art the King of Israel.

Jesus answered and said unto him, Because I said unto thee, I saw thee under the fig tree, believest thou? thou shalt see greater things than these.

And he saith unto him, Verily, verily, I say unto you, Hereafter ye shall see heaven open, and the angels of God ascending and descending upon the Son of man.

—John 1:43–51

The angel of the Lord spake unto Philip, saying, Arise, and go toward the south unto the way that goeth down from Jerusalem unto Gaza, which is desert.

And he arose and went: and, behold, a man of Ethiopia, an eunuch of great authority under Candace queen of the Ethiopians, who had the charge of all her treasure, and had come to Jerusalem for to worship,

Was returning, and sitting in his chariot read Esaias the prophet.

Then the Spirit said unto Philip, Go near, and join thyself to this chariot.

And Philip ran thither to him, and heard him read the prophet Esaias, and said, Understandest thou what thou readest?

And he said, How can I, except some man should guide me? And he desired Philip that he would come up and sit with him.

The place of the scripture which he read was this, He was led as a sheep to the slaughter; and like a lamb dumb before his shearer, so opened he not his mouth:

In his humiliation his judgment was taken away: and who shall declare his generation? for his life is taken from the earth.

And the eunuch answered Philip, and said, I pray thee, of whom speaketh the prophet this? of himself, or of some other man?

Then Philip opened his mouth, and began at the same scripture, and preached unto him Jesus.

And as they went on their way, they came unto a certain water: and the eunuch said, See, here is water; what doth hinder me to be baptized?

And Philip said, If thou believest with all thine heart, thou mayest. And he answered and said, I believe that Jesus Christ is the Son of God.

And he commanded the chariot to stand still: and they went down both into the water, both Philip and the eunuch; and he baptized him.

And when they were come up out of the water, the Spirit of the Lord caught away Philip, that the eunuch saw him no more: and he went on his way rejoicing.

—Acts 8:26–39

A Teachable Man

Let no man despise thy youth; but be thou an example of the believers, in word, in conversation, in charity, in spirit, in faith, in purity.

—1 Timothy 4:12

Paul, an apostle of Jesus Christ by the will of God, according to the promise of life which is in Christ Jesus,

To Timothy, my dearly beloved son: Grace, mercy, and peace, from God the Father and Christ Jesus our Lord.

I thank God, whom I serve from my forefathers with pure conscience, that without ceasing I have remembrance of thee in my prayers night and day;

—2 Timothy 1:1–3

Thou therefore, my son, be strong in the grace that is in Christ Jesus.

And the things that thou hast heard of me among many witnesses, the same commit thou to faithful men, who shall be able to teach others also.

Thou therefore endure hardness, as a good soldier of Jesus Christ.

—*2 Timothy 2:1–3*

But thou hast fully known my doctrine, manner of life, purpose, faith, longsuffering, charity, patience,

Persecutions, afflictions, which came unto me at Antioch, at Iconium, at Lystra; what persecutions I endured: but out of them all the Lord delivered me.

—*2 Timothy 3:10–11*

Beware of Corrupt Leaders

Virtuous men do good by setting themselves up as models before the public. But I do good by setting myself up as a warning.

—*Michel de Montaigne*

And art confident that thou thyself art a guide of the blind, a light of them which are in darkness,

An instructor of the foolish, a teacher of babes, which hast the form of knowledge and of the truth in the law.

Thou therefore which teachest another, teachest thou not thyself? thou that preachest a man should not steal, dost thou steal?

Thou that sayest a man should not commit adultery, dost thou commit adultery? thou that abhorrest idols, dost thou commit sacrilege?

Thou that makest thy boast of the law, through breaking the law dishonourest thou God?

For the name of God is blasphemed among the Gentiles through you, as it is written.

For circumcision verily profiteth, if thou keep the law: but if thou be a breaker of the law, thy circumcision is made uncircumcision.

—*Romans 2:19–25*

I marvel that ye are so soon removed from him that called you into the grace of Christ unto another gospel:

Which is not another; but there be some that trouble you, and would pervert the gospel of Christ.

But though we, or an angel from heaven, preach any other gospel unto you than that which we have preached unto you, let him be accursed.

—*Galatians 1:6–8*

Beloved, believe not every spirit, but try the spirits whether they are of God: because many false prophets are gone out into the world.

Hereby know ye the Spirit of God: Every spirit that confesseth that Jesus Christ is come in the flesh is of God:

And every spirit that confesseth not that Jesus Christ is come in the flesh is not of God: and this is that spirit of antichrist, whereof ye have heard that it should come; and even now already is it in the world.

Ye are of God, little children, and have overcome them: because greater is he that is in you, than he that is in the world.

They are of the world: therefore speak they of the world, and the world heareth them.

—*1 John 4:1–5*

Is My Devotional Life Staying Strong?

What will be the most significant moments in your day today? The time spent working, planning, worrying, socializing? Or will it be those few moments focusing on the presence of God in your life? Suppose those moments were expanded into an attitude of awareness pervading your day? Recognizing and conversing with the God who is always there—what could be more important?

Maintain a Daily "Quiet Time"

I tell you this: one loving blind desire for God alone is more valuable in itself, more pleasing to God and to the saints, more beneficial to your own growth, and more helpful to your friends, both living and dead, than anything else you could do.

—The Cloud of Unknowing

Better is an handful with quietness, than both the hands full with travail and vexation of spirit.

—*Ecclesiastes 4:6*

Be still, and know that I am God:
I will be exalted among the heathen,
I will be exalted in the earth.

—*Psalm 46:10*

Let the words of my mouth, and the meditation of my heart, be acceptable in thy sight, O LORD, my strength, and my redeemer.

—*Psalm 19:14*

How precious also are thy thoughts unto me, O God! how great is the sum of them!

If I should count them, they are more in number than the sand: when I awake, I am still with thee.

—*Psalm 139:17–18*

Spend Time in the Word

The Bible is a window in this prison of hope, through which we look into eternity.

—*John Sullivan Dwight*

Thy word is a lamp unto my feet, and a light unto my path.

I have sworn, and I will perform it, that I will keep thy righteous judgments.

I am afflicted very much: quicken me, O LORD, according unto thy word.

Accept, I beseech thee, the freewill offerings of my mouth, O LORD, and teach me thy judgments.

My soul is continually in my hand: yet do I not forget thy law.

The wicked have laid a snare for me: yet I erred not from thy precepts.

Thy testimonies have I taken as an heritage for ever: for they are the rejoicing of my heart.

I have inclined mine heart to perform thy statutes alway, even unto the end.

I hate vain thoughts: but thy law do I love.

Thou art my hiding place and my shield: I hope in thy word.

Depart from me, ye evildoers: for I will keep the commandments of my God.

Uphold me according unto thy word, that I may live: and let me not be ashamed of my hope.

—*Psalm 119:105–115*

For the word of God is quick, and powerful, and sharper than any twoedged sword, piercing even to the dividing asunder of soul and spirit, and of the joints and marrow, and is a discerner of the thoughts and intents of the heart.

Neither is there any creature that is not manifest in his sight: but all things are naked and opened unto the eyes of him with whom we have to do.

—*Hebrews 4:12–13*

Pursue Obedience in Everything

He who is false to the present duty breaks a thread in the loom, and you will see the effect when the weaving of a lifetime is unravelled.

—*William Ellery Channing*

And now, Israel, what doth the LORD thy God require of thee, but to fear the LORD thy God, to walk in all his ways, and to love him, and to serve the LORD thy God with all thy heart and with all thy soul,

To keep the commandments of the LORD, and his statutes, which I command thee this day for thy good?

—*Deuteronomy 10:12–13*

Ye are the light of the world. A city that is set on an hill cannot be hid.

Neither do men light a candle, and put it under a bushel, but on a candlestick; and it giveth light unto all that are in the house.

Let your light so shine before men, that they may see your good works, and glorify your Father which is in heaven.

—*Matthew 5:14–16*

Blessed are the undefiled in the way, who walk in the law of the LORD.

Blessed are they that keep his testimonies, and that seek him with the whole heart.

They also do no iniquity: they walk in his ways.

Thou hast commanded us to keep thy precepts diligently.

O that my ways were directed to keep thy statutes!

—*Psalm 119:1–5*

The night is far spent, the day is at hand: let us therefore cast off the works of darkness, and let us put on the armour of light.

Let us walk honestly, as in the day; not in rioting and drunkenness, not in chambering and wantonness, not in strife and envying.

But put ye on the Lord Jesus Christ, and make not provision for the flesh, to fulfil the lusts thereof.

—*Romans 13:12–14*

I, therefore, the prisoner of the Lord, beseech you that ye walk worthy of the vocation wherewith ye are called,

With all lowliness and meekness, with longsuffering, forbearing one another in love.

—*Ephesians 4:1–2*

Having your conversation honest among the Gentiles: that, whereas they speak against you as evildoers, they may by your good works, which they shall behold, glorify God in the day of visitation.

Submit yourselves to every ordinance of man for the Lord's sake: whether it be to the king, as supreme;

Or unto governors, as unto them that are sent by him for the punishment of evildoers, and for the praise of them that do well.

For so is the will of God, that with well doing ye may put to silence the ignorance of foolish men.

—*1 Peter 2:12–15*

Keep the Conversation Going: Through Prayer

God puts our prayers like rose-leaves between the leaves of His book of remembrance, and when the volume is opened at last, there shall be a precious fragrance springing from them.

—*R.G. Lee[1]*

Thou shalt make thy prayer unto him, and he shall hear thee, and thou shalt pay thy vows.

Thou shalt also decree a thing, and it shall be established unto thee: and the light shall shine upon thy ways.

—*Job 22:27–28*

For we are saved by hope: but hope that is seen is not hope: for what a man seeth, why doth he yet hope for?

But if we hope for that we see not, then do we with patience wait for it.

Likewise the Spirit also helpeth our infirmities: for we know not what we should pray for as we ought: but the Spirit itself maketh intercession for us with groanings which cannot be uttered.

And he that searcheth the hearts knoweth what is the mind of the Spirit, because he maketh intercession for the saints according to the will of God.

And we know that all things work together for good to them that love God, to them who are the called according to his purpose.

—*Romans 8:24–28*

Be careful for nothing; but in every thing by prayer and supplication with thanksgiving let your requests be made known unto God.

—*Philippians 4:6*

Let us therefore come boldly unto the throne of grace, that we may obtain mercy, and find grace to help in time of need.

—*Hebrews 4:16*

And whatsoever we ask, we receive of him, because we keep his commandments, and do those things that are pleasing in his sight.

—*1 John 3:22*

These things have I written unto you that believe on the name of the Son of God; that ye may know that ye have eternal life, and that ye may believe on the name of the Son of God.

And this is the confidence that we have in him, that, if we ask any thing according to his will, he heareth us:

And if we know that he hear us, whatsoever we ask, we know that we have the petitions that we desired of him.

—*1 John 5:13–15*

Pray without ceasing.

—*1 Thessalonians 5:17*

Strengthen Your Personal Witness

To be a witness does not consist in engaging in propaganda, nor even in stirring people up; but in being a living mystery. It means to live in such a way that one's life would not make sense if God did not exist.[2]

Whosoever shall confess me before men, him shall the Son of man also confess before the angels of God:

But he that denieth me before men shall be denied before the angels of God.

—*Luke 12:8–9*

No man, when he hath lighted a candle, covereth it with a vessel, or putteth it under a bed; but setteth it on a candlestick, that they which enter in may see the light. . . .

Now the man out of whom the devils were departed besought him that he might be with him: but Jesus sent him away, saying,

Return to thine own house, and shew how great things God hath done unto thee. And he went his way, and published throughout the

whole city how great things Jesus had done
unto him.

—*Luke 8:16, 38–39*

For I will not dare to speak of any of those
things which Christ hath not wrought by me, to
make the Gentiles obedient, by word and deed,

Through mighty signs and wonders, by the
power of the Spirit of God; so that from Jerusalem, and round about unto Illyricum, I have
fully preached the gospel of Christ.

Yea, so have I strived to preach the gospel,
not where Christ was named, lest I should
build upon another man's foundation:

But as it is written, To whom he was not
spoken of, they shall see: and they that have
not heard shall understand.

—*Romans 15:18–21*

Stand Firm against Temptation

Better shun the bait than struggle in the snare.
—John Dryden

And it came to pass after these things, that his master's wife cast her eyes upon Joseph; and she said, Lie with me.

But he refused, and said unto his master's wife, Behold, my master wotteth not what is with me in the house, and he hath committed all that he hath to my hand;

There is none greater in this house than I; neither hath he kept back any thing from me but thee, because thou art his wife: how then can I do this great wickedness, and sin against God?

And it came to pass, as she spake to Joseph day by day, that he hearkened not unto her, to lie by her, or to be with her.

—Genesis 39:7–10

There hath no temptation taken you but such as is common to man: but God is faithful, who will not suffer you to be tempted above that ye are able; but will with the temptation also make a way to escape, that ye may be able to bear it.

—1 Corinthians 10:13

For the weapons of our warfare are not carnal, but mighty through God to the pulling down of strong holds.

—2 Corinthians 10:4

Put on the whole armour of God, that ye may be able to stand against the wiles of the devil.

For we wrestle not against flesh and blood, but against principalities, against powers, against the rulers of the darkness of this world, against spiritual wickedness in high places.

Wherefore take unto you the whole armour of God, that ye may be able to withstand in the evil day, and having done all, to stand.

Stand therefore, having your loins girt about with truth, and having on the breastplate of righteousness.

—Ephesians 6:11–14

But the Lord is faithful, who shall stablish you, and keep you from evil.

—2 Thessalonians 3:3

The Lord shall deliver me from every evil work, and will preserve me unto his heavenly kingdom: to whom be glory for ever and ever. Amen.

—*2 Timothy 4:18*

Forasmuch then as the children are partakers of flesh and blood, he also himself likewise took part of the same; that through death he might destroy him that had the power of death, that is, the devil;

And deliver them who through fear of death were all their lifetime subject to bondage.

For verily he took not on him the nature of angels; but he took on him the seed of Abraham.

Wherefore in all things it behoved him to be made like unto his brethren, that he might be a merciful and faithful high priest in things pertaining to God, to make reconciliation for the sins of the people.

For in that he himself hath suffered being tempted, he is able to succour them that are tempted.

Wherefore, holy brethren, partakers of the heavenly calling, consider the Apostle and High Priest of our profession, Christ Jesus.

—*Hebrews 2:14–18; 3:1*

Watch therefore: for ye know not what hour your Lord doth come.

But know this, that if the goodman of the house had known in what watch the thief would come, he would have watched, and would not have suffered his house to be broken up.

Therefore be ye also ready: for in such an hour as ye think not the Son of man cometh.

—*Matthew 24:42–44*

Then saith [Jesus] unto them, My soul is exceeding sorrowful, even unto death: tarry ye here, and watch with me.

And he went a little farther, and fell on his face, and prayed, saying, O my Father, if it be possible, let this cup pass from me: nevertheless not as I will, but as thou wilt.

And he cometh unto the disciples, and findeth them asleep, and saith unto Peter, What, could ye not watch with me one hour?

Watch and pray, that ye enter not into temptation: the spirit indeed is willing, but the flesh is weak.

He went away again the second time, and prayed, saying, O my Father, if this cup may not pass away from me, except I drink it, thy will be done.

Matthew 26:38–42

Depend on God's Strength Each Day . . .

Paul's word for [the] gradual transformation of a sow's ear into a silk purse is sanctification, and he sees it as the second stage in the process of salvation. Being sanctified is a long and painful stage because with part of themselves sinners prefer their sin, just as with part of himself the Beast prefers his glistening snout and curved tusks. Many drop out with the job hardly more than begun, and among those who stay with it there are few if any who don't drag their feet most of the way.

—Frederick Buechner [3]

When thou goest, thy steps shall not be straitened; and when thou runnest, thou shalt not stumble.

—Proverbs 4:12

Ask, and it shall be given you; seek, and ye shall find; knock, and it shall be opened unto you.

—Matthew 7:7

I beseech you therefore, brethren, by the mercies of God, that ye present your bodies a living sacrifice, holy, acceptable unto God, which is your reasonable service.

—*Romans 12:1*

. . . And Live by His Spirit, Moment by Moment

Sufficient to each day are the duties to be done and the trials to be endured. God never built a Christian strong enough to carry today's duties and tomorrow's anxieties piled on top of them.

—*Theodore Ledyard Cuyler*

If ye then, being evil, know how to give good gifts unto your children: how much more shall your heavenly Father give the Holy Spirit to them that ask him?

—*Luke 11:13*

In the last day, that great day of the feast, Jesus stood and cried, saying, If any man thirst, let him come unto me, and drink.

He that believeth on me, as the scripture hath said, out of his belly shall flow rivers of living water.

(But this spake he of the Spirit, which they that believe on him should receive: for the Holy Ghost was not yet given; because that Jesus was not yet glorified.)

—John 7:37–39

And I will pray the Father, and he shall give you another Comforter, that he may abide with you for ever;

Even the Spirit of truth; whom the world cannot receive, because it seeth him not, neither knoweth him: but ye know him; for he dwelleth with you, and shall be in you.

—John 14:16–17

Five

Suppose I'm Looking for Love?

Sometimes it's easy to forget that everyone experiences loneliness. At times you may feel you're the only one "left out in the cold." And it may seem as though having more friends, or even getting married, will be the cure.

But no matter how many people we gather around us, we still need the most fulfilling relationship of all—fellowship with our Creator. That is what we were made for, what all our longing really means.

Filled with Loneliness?

There is a tendency in each one of us to deny loneliness. We want to live life independently, no leaning on other people. But a nagging sense of loneliness keeps getting in the way. Sometimes it becomes so severe we can hardly think about anything else. I believe God created us incomplete, not as a cruel trick to edge us toward self-pity, but as an opportunity to edge us toward others with similar needs.

—*Phillip Yancey* [1]

He hath put my brethren far from me, and mine acquaintance are verily estranged from me.

My kinsfolk have failed, and my familiar friends have forgotten me.

—*Job 19:13–14*

Thou hast put away mine acquaintance far from me; thou hast made me an abomination unto them: I am shut up, and I cannot come forth.

—*Psalm 88:8*

For a small moment have I forsaken thee;
but with great mercies will I gather thee.

—*Isaiah 54:7*

Seek Out Christian Fellowship

*The disciples call upon the heavenly Father as
a corporate body. They call upon a Father who
already knows his children's needs. The call of
Jesus binds them into a brotherhood. In Jesus
they have apprehended the lovingkindness of
the Father. In the name of the Son of God they
are privileged to call God Father. They are on
earth, and their Father is in heaven, He looks
down on them from above, and they lift up
their eyes to him.*

— *Deitrich Bonhoeffer* [2]

Let us consider one another to provoke
unto love and to good works:

Not forsaking the assembling of ourselves
together, as the manner of some is; but
exhorting one another: and so much the
more, as ye see the day approaching.

—*Hebrews 10:24–25*

We then that are strong ought to bear the infirmities of the weak, and not to please ourselves.

Let every one of us please his neighbour for his good to edification.

For even Christ pleased not himself; but, as it is written, The reproaches of them that reproached thee fell on me.

For whatsoever things were written aforetime were written for our learning, that we through patience and comfort of the scriptures might have hope.

Now the God of patience and consolation grant you to be likeminded one toward another according to Christ Jesus:

That ye may with one mind and one mouth glorify God, even the Father of our Lord Jesus Christ.

Wherefore receive ye one another, as Christ also received us to the glory of God.

—*Romans 15:1–7*

For ye are all the children of God by faith in Christ Jesus.

For as many of you as have been baptized into Christ have put on Christ.

There is neither Jew nor Greek, there is neither bond nor free, there is neither male nor female: for ye are all one in Christ Jesus.

—*Galatians 3:26–28*

Let brotherly love continue.

—*Hebrews 13:1*

. . . Or Get Married!

The goal of our life should not be to find joy in marriage, but to bring more love and truth into the world. We marry to assist each other in this task. The most selfish and hateful life of all is that of two beings who unite in order to enjoy life. The highest calling is that of the man who has dedicated his life to serving God and doing good, and who unites with a woman in order to further that purpose.

—*Leo Tolstoy* [3]

Marriage is honourable in all, and the bed undefiled.

—*Hebrews 13:4a*

So God created man in his own image, in the image of God created he him; male and female created he them.

—*Genesis 1:27*

The LORD God said, It is not good that the man should be alone; I will make him an help meet for him.

And out of the ground the LORD God formed every beast of the field, and every fowl of the air; and brought them unto Adam to see what he would call them: and whatsoever Adam called every living creature, that was the name thereof.

And Adam gave names to all cattle, and to the fowl of the air, and to every beast of the field; but for Adam there was not found an help meet for him.

And the LORD God caused a deep sleep to fall upon Adam and he slept: and he took one of his ribs, and closed up the flesh instead thereof;

And the rib, which the LORD God had taken from man, made he a woman, and brought her unto the man.

And Adam said, This is now bone of my bones, and flesh of my flesh: she shall be called Woman, because she was taken out of Man.

Therefore shall a man leave his father and his mother, and shall cleave unto his wife: and they shall be one flesh.

And they were both naked, the man and his wife, and were not ashamed.

—*Genesis 2:18–25*

So Boaz took Ruth, and she was his wife: and when he went in unto her, the LORD gave her conception, and she bare a son.

And the women said unto Naomi, Blessed be the LORD, which hath not left thee this day without a kinsman, that his name may be famous in Israel.

And he shall be unto thee a restorer of thy life, and a nourisher of thine old age: for thy daughter in law, which loveth thee, which is better to thee than seven sons, hath born him.

—*Ruth 4:13–15*

When a man hath taken a new wife, he shall not go out to war, neither shall he be charged with any business: but he shall be free

at home one year, and shall cheer up his wife
which he hath taken.

—*Deuteronomy 24:5*

Remember: Romance Was God's Idea

My beloved is white and ruddy, the chiefest
among ten thousand.

His head is as the most fine gold, his locks
are bushy, and black as a raven.

His eyes are as the eyes of doves by the rivers of waters, washed with milk, and fitly set.

His cheeks are as a bed of spices, as sweet
flowers: his lips like lilies, dropping sweet
smelling myrrh.

His hands are as gold rings set with the
beryl: his belly is as bright ivory overlaid with
sapphires.

His legs are as pillars of marble, set upon
sockets of fine gold: his countenance is as
Lebanon, excellent as the cedars.

His mouth is most sweet: yea, he is altogether lovely. This is my beloved, and this is
my friend, O daughters of Jerusalem.

—*Song of Solomon 5:10–16*

Make haste, my beloved, and be thou like to a roe or to a young hart upon the mountains of spices.

—*Song of Solomon 8:14*

🏷 *But Commit to Sexual Faithfulness*

Live joyfully with the wife whom thou lovest all the days of the life of thy vanity, which he hath given thee under the sun, all the days of thy vanity: for that is thy portion in this life, and in thy labour which thou takest under the sun.

—*Ecclesiastes 9:9*

Ye have heard that it was said by them of old time, Thou shalt not commit adultery:

But I say unto you, That whosoever looketh on a woman to lust after her hath committed adultery with her already in his heart.

—*Matthew 5:27–28*

Likewise reckon ye also yourselves to be dead indeed unto sin, but alive unto God through Jesus Christ our Lord.

Let not sin therefore reign in your mortal body, that ye should obey it in the lusts thereof.

Neither yield ye your members as instruments of unrighteousness unto sin: but yield yourselves unto God, as those that are alive from the dead, and your members as instruments of righteousness unto God.

For sin shall not have dominion over you: for ye are not under the law, but under grace.

—Romans 6:11–14

For this is the will of God, even your sanctification, that ye should abstain from fornication:

That every one of you should know how to possess his vessel in sanctification and honour;

Not in the lust of concupiscence, even as the Gentiles which know not God:

That no man go beyond and defraud his brother in any matter: because that the Lord is the avenger of all such, as we also have forewarned you and testified.

For God hath not called us unto uncleanness, but unto holiness.

He therefore that despiseth, despiseth not man, but God, who hath also given unto us his holy Spirit.

—1 Thessalonians 4:3–8

Flee also youthful lusts: but follow righteousness, faith, charity, peace, with them that call on the Lord out of a pure heart.

—2 Timothy 2:22

And Make Marriage the Best It Can Be

Let thy fountain be blessed: and rejoice with the wife of thy youth.

Let her be as the loving hind and pleasant roe; let her breasts satisfy thee at all times; and be thou ravished always with her love.

And why wilt thou, my son, be ravished with a strange woman, and embrace the bosom of a stranger?

—Proverbs 5:18–20

House and riches are the inheritance of fathers: and a prudent wife is from the LORD.

—*Proverbs 19:14*

Then will I cause to cease from the cities of Judah, and from the streets of Jerusalem, the voice of mirth, and the voice of gladness, the voice of the bridegroom, and the voice of the bride: for the land shall be desolate.

—*Jeremiah 7:34*

Lonely or Not, Keep Reaching Out to Others

Strength to bear is found in duty alone. And he is blest indeed who learns to make the joy of others cure his own heartache.

—*Sir Francis Drake*

Then Jesus six days before the passover came to Bethany, where Lazarus was which had been dead, whom he raised from the dead.

There they made him a supper; and Martha served: but Lazarus was one of them that sat at the table with him.

Then took Mary a pound of ointment of spikenard, very costly, and anointed the feet of Jesus, and wiped his feet with her hair: and the house was filled with the odour of the ointment.

Then saith one of his disciples, Judas Iscariot, Simon's son, which should betray him,

Why was not this ointment sold for three hundred pence, and given to the poor?

This he said, not that he cared for the poor; but because he was a thief, and had the bag, and bare what was put therein.

Then said Jesus, Let her alone: against the day of my burying hath she kept this.

—*John 12:1–7*

Bear ye one another's burdens, and so fulfil the law of Christ.

For if a man think himself to be something, when he is nothing, he deceiveth himself.

But let every man prove his own work, and then shall he have rejoicing in himself alone, and not in another.

—*Galatians 6:2–4*

With all lowliness and meekness, with longsuffering, forbearing one another in love;

Endeavouring to keep the unity of the Spirit in the bond of peace.

—Ephesians 4:2–3

Find Fulfillment in Your Relationship with God

Our whole being by its very nature is one vast need; incomplete, preparatory, empty yet cluttered, crying out for Him who can untie things that are now knotted together and tie up things that are still dangling loose.

—C. S. Lewis

Whoso trusteth in the LORD, happy is he.

—Proverbs 16:20b

Acquaint now thyself with him, and be at peace: thereby good shall come unto thee.

Receive, I pray thee, the law from his mouth, and lay up his words in thine heart.

If thou return to the Almighty, thou shalt be built up, thou shalt put away iniquity far from thy tabernacles.

Then shalt thou lay up gold as dust, and the gold of Ophir as the stones of the brooks.

Yea, the Almighty shall be thy defence, and thou shalt have plenty of silver.

For then shalt thou have thy delight in the Almighty, and shalt lift up thy face unto God.

—Job 22:21–26

Happy art thou, O Israel: who is like unto thee, O people saved by the LORD, the shield of thy help, and who is the sword of thy excellency! and thine enemies shall be found liars unto thee; and thou shalt tread upon their high places.

—Deuteronomy 33:29

They shall be abundantly satisfied with the fatness of thy house; and thou shalt make them drink of the river of thy pleasures.

—Psalm 36:8

I delight to do thy will, O my God: yea, thy law is within my heart.

—Psalm 40:8

My soul shall be satisfied as with marrow and fatness; and my mouth shall praise thee with joyful lips.

—Psalm 63:5

Blessed is every one that feareth the LORD; that walketh in his ways.

For thou shalt eat the labour of thine hands: happy shalt thou be, and it shall be well with thee.

—Psalm 128:1–2

Happy is that people, that is in such a case: yea, happy is that people, whose God is the LORD.

—Psalm 144:15

Does God Care About My Troubles?

Nobody ever said life would be easy. Certainly, Jesus never said it! "In this world you will have tribulations." The key is to respond in ways that bring new growth and a deeper faith in God's sovereignty. It is possible, knowing that Christ is with us, every step of the way. And remember: He also said, "I have overcome the world."

In Times of Trouble . . .

God gives burdens,
also shoulders.

—*Yiddish proverb*

Many are the afflictions of the righteous:
but the LORD delivereth him out of them all.

—*Psalm 34:19*

He shall deliver thee in six troubles: yea, in
seven there shall no evil touch thee.

—*Job 5:19*

And we know that all things work together
for good to them that love God, to them who
are the called according to his purpose.

—*Romans 8:28*

We are troubled on every side, yet not dis-
tressed; we are perplexed, but not in despair;

Persecuted, but not forsaken; cast down,
but not destroyed.

—*2 Corinthians 4:8–9*

When You're Afraid

O friend, never strike sail to a fear! Come into port greatly, or sail with God the seas.

—*Ralph Waldo Emerson*

Therefore will not we fear, though the earth be removed, and though the mountains be carried into the midst of the sea.

Psalm 46:2

Hearken unto me, ye that know righteousness, the people in whose heart is my law; fear ye not the reproach of men, neither be ye afraid of their revilings.

—*Isaiah 51:7*

For God hath not given us the spirit of fear; but of power, and of love, and of a sound mind.

—*2 Timothy 1:7*

There is no fear in love; but perfect love casteth out fear: because fear hath torment. He that feareth is not made perfect in love.

—*1 John 4:18*

When You Feel Depressed

It becomes no one to nurse despair, but, in the teeth of clenched antagonisms, to follow up the worthiest till he die.

—*Alfred, Lord Tennyson*

Have mercy upon me, O LORD; for I am weak: O LORD, heal me; for my bones are vexed.

My soul is also sore vexed: but thou, O LORD, how long?

—*Psalm 6:2–3*

Come unto me, all ye that labour and are heavy laden, and I will give you rest.

Take my yoke upon you, and learn of me; for I am meek and lowly in heart: and ye shall find rest unto your souls.

For my yoke is easy, and my burden is light.

—*Matthew 11:28–30*

But God hath chosen the foolish things of the world to confound the wise; and God hath chosen the weak things of the world to confound the things which are mighty.

—*1 Corinthians 1:27*

[The Lord] said unto me, My grace is sufficient for thee: for my strength is made perfect in weakness. Most gladly therefore will I rather glory in my infirmities, that the power of Christ may rest upon me.

Therefore I take pleasure in infirmities, in reproaches, in necessities, in persecutions, in distresses for Christ's sake: for when I am weak, then am I strong.

—*2 Corinthians 12:9–10*

When You're Worried

Worry gives a small thing a big shadow.
—*Swedish Proverb*

Thou wilt keep him in perfect peace, whose mind is stayed on thee: because he trusteth in thee.

—*Isaiah 26:3*

Blessed is the man that trusteth in the LORD, and whose hope the LORD is. For he shall be as a tree planted by the waters, and that spreadeth out her roots by the river, and shall not see when heat cometh, but her leaf shall be green; and shall not be careful in the year of drought, neither shall cease from yielding fruit.

—*Jeremiah 17:7–8*

Peace I leave with you, my peace I give unto you: not as the world giveth, give I unto you. Let not your heart be troubled, neither let it be afraid.

—*John 14:27*

Now the Lord of peace himself give you peace always by all means. The Lord be with you all.

—*2 Thessalonians 3:16*

When You Struggle with Doubt

Our doubts are traitors,
and make us lose the good
we oft might win
by fearing to attempt.

—*William Shakespeare*

Behold, I am the LORD, the God of all flesh: is there any thing too hard for me?

—*Jeremiah 32:27*

For verily I say unto you, That whosoever shall say unto this mountain, Be thou removed, and be thou cast into the sea; and shall not doubt in his heart, but shall believe that those things which he saith shall come to pass; he shall have whatsoever he saith.

—*Mark 11:23*

Let us hold fast the profession of our faith without wavering; (for he is faithful that promised). . . .

Cast not away therefore your confidence, which hath great recompence of reward.

For ye have need of patience, that, after ye have done the will of God, ye might receive the promise.

For yet a little while, and he that shall come will come, and will not tarry.

—*Hebrews 10:23, 35–37*

And this is the confidence that we have in him, that, if we ask any thing according to his will, he heareth us:

And if we know that he hear us, whatsoever we ask, we know that we have the petitions that we desired of him.

—*1 John 5:14–15*

For with God nothing shall be impossible.

—*Luke 1:37*

When You Feel Tempted

It is easier to stay out than get out.

—*Mark Twain*

Make not provision for the flesh, to fulfil the lusts thereof.

—*Romans 13:14b*

The Lord knoweth how to deliver the godly out of temptations, and to reserve the unjust unto the day of judgment to be punished.

—*2 Peter 2:9*

The LORD shall preserve thee from all evil: he shall preserve thy soul.

The LORD shall preserve thy going out and thy coming in from this time forth, and even for evermore.

—*Psalm 121:7–8*

Rejoice not against me, O mine enemy: when I fall, I shall arise; when I sit in darkness, the LORD shall be a light unto me.

—*Micah 7:8*

For the weapons of our warfare are not carnal, but mighty through God to the pulling down of strong holds.

—*2 Corinthians 10:4*

But the Lord is faithful, who shall stablish you, and keep you from evil.

—*2 Thessalonians 3:3*

The Lord shall deliver me from every evil work, and will preserve me unto his heavenly kingdom: to whom be glory for ever and ever. Amen.

—*2 Timothy 4:18*

Recall the Power of Christ . . .

Jesus! the name high over all,
In hell, or earth, or sky;
Angels and men before it fall,
And devils fear and fly.

—*Charles Wesley*

When my soul fainted within me I remembered the LORD: and my prayer came in unto thee.

—*Jonah 2:7a*

Who is the image of the invisible God, the firstborn of every creature:

For by him were all things created, that are in heaven, and that are in earth, visible and invisible, whether they be thrones, or dominions, or principalities, or powers: all things were created by him, and for him:

And he is before all things, and by him all things consist.

And he is the head of the body, the church: who is the beginning, the firstborn from the dead; that in all things he might have the preeminence.

For it pleased the Father that in him should all fulness dwell.

—*Colossians 1:15–19*

 His Power to Heal You

Jesus went up to Jerusalem.

Now there is at Jerusalem by the sheep market a pool, which is called in the Hebrew tongue Bethesda, having five porches.

In these lay a great multitude of impotent folk, of blind, halt, withered, waiting for the moving of the water.

For an angel went down at a certain season into the pool, and troubled the water: whosoever then first after the troubling of the water stepped in was made whole of whatsoever disease he had.

And a certain man was there, which had an infirmity thirty and eight years.

When Jesus saw him lie, and knew that he had been now a long time in that case, he saith unto him, Wilt thou be made whole?

The impotent man answered him, Sir, I have no man, when the water is troubled, to put me into the pool: but while I am coming, another steppeth down before me.

Jesus saith unto him, Rise, take up thy bed, and walk.

And immediately the man was made whole, and took up his bed, and walked: and on the same day was the sabbath.

The Jews therefore said unto him that was cured, It is the sabbath day: it is not lawful for thee to carry thy bed.

He answered them, He that made me whole, the same said unto me, Take up thy bed, and walk.

Then asked they him, What man is that which said unto thee, Take up thy bed, and walk?

And he that was healed wist not who it was: for Jesus had conveyed himself away, a multitude being in that place.

Afterward Jesus findeth him in the temple, and said unto him, Behold, thou art made whole: sin no more, lest a worse thing come unto thee.

The man departed, and told the Jews that it was Jesus, which had made him whole.

And therefore did the Jews persecute Jesus, and sought to slay him, because he had done these things on the sabbath day.

—John 5:1–16

His Power over All Spiritual Opposition

When [Jesus] came to his disciples, he saw a great multitude about them, and the scribes questioning with them.

And straightway all the people, when they beheld him, were greatly amazed, and running to him saluted him.

And he asked the scribes, What question ye with them?

And one of the multitude answered and said, Master, I have brought unto thee my son, which hath a dumb spirit;

And wheresoever he taketh him, he teareth him: and he foameth, and gnasheth with his teeth, and pineth away: and I spake to thy disciples that they should cast him out; and they could not.

He answereth him, and saith, O faithless generation, how long shall I be with you? how long shall I suffer you? bring him unto me.

And they brought him unto him: and when he saw him, straightway the spirit tare him; and he fell on the ground, and wallowed foaming.

And he asked his father, How long is it ago since this came unto him? And he said, Of a child.

And ofttimes it hath cast him into the fire, and into the waters, to destroy him: but if thou canst do any thing, have compassion on us, and help us.

Jesus said unto him, If thou canst believe, all things are possible to him that believeth.

And straightway the father of the child cried out, and said with tears, Lord, I believe; help thou mine unbelief.

When Jesus saw that the people came running together, he rebuked the foul spirit, saying unto him, Thou dumb and deaf spirit, I charge thee, come out of him, and enter no more into him.

And the spirit cried, and rent him sore, and came out of him: and he was as one dead; insomuch that many said, He is dead.

But Jesus took him by the hand, and lifted him up; and he arose.

And when he was come into the house, his disciples asked him privately, Why could not we cast him out?

And he said unto them, This kind can come forth by nothing, but by prayer and fasting.

—*Mark 9:14–29*

His Power for Practical Compassion

In those days the multitude being very great, and having nothing to eat, Jesus called his disciples unto him, and saith unto them,

I have compassion on the multitude, because they have now been with me three days, and have nothing to eat:

And if I send them away fasting to their own houses, they will faint by the way: for divers of them came from far.

And his disciples answered him, From whence can a man satisfy these men with bread here in the wilderness?

And he asked them, How many loaves have ye? And they said, Seven.

And he commanded the people to sit down on the ground: and he took the seven loaves, and gave thanks, and brake, and gave to his disciples to set before them; and they did set them before the people.

And they had a few small fishes: and he blessed, and commanded to set them also before them.

So they did eat, and were filled: and they took up of the broken meat that was left seven baskets.

And they that had eaten were about four thousand: and he sent them away.

—*Mark 8:1–9*

His Power Over Death Itself

And it came to pass the day after, that [Jesus] went into a city called Nain; and many of his disciples went with him, and much people.

Now when he came nigh to the gate of the city, behold, there was a dead man carried out, the only son of his mother, and she was a widow: and much people of the city was with her.

And when the Lord saw her, he had compassion on her, and said unto her, Weep not.

And he came and touched the bier: and they that bare him stood still. And he said, Young man, I say unto thee, Arise.

And he that was dead sat up, and began to speak. And he delivered him to his mother.

And there came a fear on all: and they glorified God, saying, That a great prophet is risen up among us; and, That God hath visited his people.

—Luke 7:11–16

In Every Trial, Invite God's Peace . . .

There was peace in their hearts. They were filled with the fearlessness of those who have lost everything, the fearlessness which is not easy to come by but which endures.

—*Alexander Solzhenitsyn*[1]

For in the time of trouble he shall hide me in his pavilion: in the secret of his tabernacle shall he hide me; he shall set me up upon a rock.

—*Psalm 27:5*

And all thy children shall be taught of the LORD; and great shall be the peace of thy children.

In righteousness shalt thou be established: thou shalt be far from oppression; for thou shalt not fear: and from terror; for it shall not come near thee.

Behold, they shall surely gather together, but not by me: whosoever shall gather together against thee shall fall for thy sake.

Behold, I have created the smith that bloweth the coals in the fire, and that bringeth forth an instrument for his work; and I have created the waster to destroy.

No weapon that is formed against thee shall prosper; and every tongue that shall rise against thee in judgment thou shalt condemn. This is the heritage of the servants of the LORD, and their righteousness is of me, saith the LORD.

—Isaiah 54:13–17

. . . And Let God Nurture You

My God, I choose the whole lot. No point in becoming a saint by halves. I'm not afraid of suffering for your sake; the only thing I'm afraid of is clinging to my own will. Take it. I want the whole lot, everything whatsoever that is your will for me.

—Therese of Lisieux

In the multitude of my thoughts within me thy comforts delight my soul.

—Psalm 94:19

For he maketh sore, and bindeth up: he woundeth, and his hands make whole.

—Job 5:18

Seven

What About My Work and Money Decisions?

It's normal to want to feel secure. No one likes wondering where the next dollar is coming from. But how can we keep that concern from taking over everything else? Perhaps knowing God's promises of provision will help. The Bible has a lot to say about work and money. Read on!

Feeling Worried About Money?

Riches are the pettiest and least worthy gifts which God can give us. What are they to God's Word, to bodily gifts, such as beauty and health; or to the gifts of the mind, such as understanding, skill, wisdom? Yet we toil for them day and night, and take not rest. Therefore God commonly gives riches to foolish people to whom he gives nothing else.
—*Martin Luther*

I am feeble and sore broken: I have roared by reason of the disquietness of my heart.
—*Psalm 38:8*

Be careful for nothing; but in every thing by prayer and supplication with thanksgiving let your requests be made known unto God.

And the peace of God, which passeth all understanding, shall keep your hearts and minds through Christ Jesus. . . .

Not that I speak in respect of want: for I have learned, in whatsoever state I am, therewith to be content.

I know both how to be abased, and I know how to abound: every where and in all things I am instructed both to be full and to be hungry, both to abound and to suffer need.

I can do all things through Christ which strengtheneth me.

—Philippians 4:6–7, 11–13

Practice Good Stewardship

The earth is the LORD's, and the fulness thereof; the world, and they that dwell therein.

For he hath founded it upon the seas, and established it upon the floods.

—Psalm 24:1–2

What? know ye not that your body is the temple of the Holy Ghost which is in you, which ye have of God, and ye are not your own?

For ye are bought with a price: therefore glorify God in your body, and in your spirit, which are God's.

—1 Corinthians 6:19–20

For I mean not that other men be eased, and ye burdened:

But by an equality, that now at this time your abundance may be a supply for their want, that their abundance also may be a supply for your want: that there may be equality:

As it is written, He that had gathered much had nothing over; and he that had gathered little had no lack.

—*2 Corinthians 8:13–15*

When James, Cephas, and John, who seemed to be pillars, perceived the grace that was given unto me, they gave to me and Barnabas the right hands of fellowship; that we should go unto the heathen, and they unto the circumcision.

Only they would that we should remember the poor; the same which I also was forward to do.

—*Galatians 2:9–10*

As every man hath received the gift, even so minister the same one to another, as good stewards of the manifold grace of God.

If any man speak, let him speak as the oracles of God; if any man minister, let him do it as of the ability which God giveth: that God in all things may be glorified through Jesus Christ, to whom be praise and dominion for ever and ever. Amen.

—1 Peter 4:10–11

Use Possessions Wisely and Frugally

A good man leaveth an inheritance to his children's children: and the wealth of the sinner is laid up for the just.

—Proverbs 13:22

He that loveth pleasure shall be a poor man: he that loveth wine and oil shall not be rich.

The wicked shall be a ransom for the righteous, and the transgressor for the upright.

It is better to dwell in the wilderness, than with a contentious and an angry woman.

There is treasure to be desired and oil in the dwelling of the wise; but a foolish man spendeth it up.

He that followeth after righteousness and mercy findeth life, righteousness, and honour.

—*Proverbs 21:17–21*

Be not among winebibbers; among riotous eaters of flesh:

For the drunkard and the glutton shall come to poverty: and drowsiness shall clothe a man with rags.

—*Proverbs 23:20–21*

And they did all eat, and were filled: and they took up of the broken meat that was left seven baskets full.

—*Matthew 15:37*

And when James, Cephas, and John, who seemed to be pillars, perceived the grace that was given unto me, they gave to me and Barnabas the right hands of fellowship; that we should go unto the heathen, and they unto the circumcision.

Only they would that we should remember the poor; the same which I also was forward to do.

Galatians 2:9–10

Welcome Hard Work

Go to the ant, thou sluggard; consider her ways, and be wise:

Which having no guide, overseer, or ruler,

Provideth her meat in the summer, and gathereth her food in the harvest.

How long wilt thou sleep, O sluggard? when wilt thou arise out of thy sleep?

Yet a little sleep, a little slumber, a little folding of the hands to sleep:

So shall thy poverty come as one that travelleth, and thy want as an armed man.

—*Proverbs 6:6–11*

He that tilleth his land shall be satisfied with bread: but he that followeth vain persons is void of understanding. . . .

The hand of the diligent shall bear rule: but the slothful shall be under tribute.

Heaviness in the heart of man maketh it stoop: but a good word maketh it glad.

The righteous is more excellent than his neighbour: but the way of the wicked seduceth them.

The slothful man roasteth not that which he took in hunting: but the substance of a diligent man is precious.

—*Proverbs 12:11, 24–27*

Be thou diligent to know the state of thy flocks, and look well to thy herds.

For riches are not for ever: and doth the crown endure to every generation?

The hay appeareth, and the tender grass sheweth itself, and herbs of the mountains are gathered.

The lambs are for thy clothing, and the goats are the price of the field.

And thou shalt have goats' milk enough for thy food, for the food of thy household, and for the maintenance for thy maidens.

—*Proverbs 27:23–27*

The ants are a people not strong, yet they prepare their meat in the summer;

The conies are but a feeble folk, yet make they their houses in the rocks;

The locusts have no king, yet go they forth all of them by bands;

The spider taketh hold with her hands, and is in kings' palaces.

—Proverbs 30:25–28

I have coveted no man's silver, or gold, or apparel.

Yea, ye yourselves know, that these hands have ministered unto my necessities, and to them that were with me.

—Acts 20:33–34

And that ye study to be quiet, and to do your own business, and to work with your own hands, as we commanded you;

That ye may walk honestly toward them that are without, and that ye may have lack of nothing.

—1 Thessalonians 4:11–12

For even when we were with you, this we commanded you, that if any would not work, neither should he eat.

For we hear that there are some which walk among you disorderly, working not at all, but are busybodies.

Now them that are such we command and exhort by our Lord Jesus Christ, that with quietness they work, and eat their own bread.

—*2 Thessalonians 3:10–12*

🎓 Avoid Untrustworthy Actions at Work

Hear another parable: There was a certain householder, which planted a vineyard, and hedged it round about, and digged a wine-press in it, and built a tower, and let it out to husbandmen, and went into a far country:

And when the time of the fruit drew near, he sent his servants to the husbandmen, that they might receive the fruits of it.

And the husbandmen took his servants, and beat one, and killed another, and stoned another.

Again, he sent other servants more than the first: and they did unto them likewise.

But last of all he sent unto them his son, saying, They will reverence my son.

But when the husbandmen saw the son, they said among themselves, This is the heir; come, let us kill him, and let us seize on his inheritance.

And they caught him, and cast him out of the vineyard, and slew him.

When the lord therefore of the vineyard cometh, what will he do unto those husbandmen?

They say unto him, He will miserably destroy those wicked men, and will let out his vineyard unto other husbandmen, which shall render him the fruits in their seasons.

—*Matthew 21:33–41*

Art thou called being a servant? care not for it: but if thou mayest be made free, use it rather.

For he that is called in the Lord, being a servant, is the Lord's freeman: likewise also he that is called, being free, is Christ's servant.

Ye are bought with a price; be not ye the servants of men.

—*1 Corinthians 7:21–23*

Rest in God's Peace

This is the longing of all mankind—to have security, to know where one's place is. God created man and then He created a place for him, the Garden of Eden. When man lost God he lost at the same time his place. Since then, the longing for a place where he belongs, where he feels at home, is in the heart of every human being. In light of this, Jesus' promise "to prepare a place" for us is filled with new meaning. Those who have found Him have found their place.

—*Walter Trobisch*[1]

Thou wilt keep him in perfect peace, whose mind is stayed on thee: because he trusteth in thee.

—*Isaiah 26:3*

For he shall be as a tree planted by the waters, and that spreadeth out her roots by the river, and shall not see when heat cometh, but her leaf shall be green; and shall not be careful in the year of drought, neither shall cease from yielding fruit.

—Jeremiah 17:8

These things I have spoken unto you, that in me ye might have peace. In the world ye shall have tribulation: but be of good cheer; I have overcome the world.

—John 16:33

But he that prophesieth speaketh unto men to edification, and exhortation, and comfort.

—1 Corinthians 14:3

For [Jesus] is our peace, who hath made both one, and hath broken down the middle wall of partition between us;

Having abolished in his flesh the enmity, even the law of commandments contained in ordinances; for to make in himself of twain one new man, so making peace;

And that he might reconcile both unto God in one body by the cross, having slain the enmity thereby:

And came and preached peace to you which were afar off, and to them that were nigh.

—Ephesians 2:14–17

And the peace of God, which passeth all understanding, shall keep your hearts and minds through Christ Jesus.

—Philippians 4:7

Now the Lord of peace himself give you peace always by all means. The Lord be with you all.

—2 Thessalonians 3:16

Six days thou shalt do thy work, and on the seventh day thou shalt rest: that thine ox and thine ass may rest, and the son of thy hand-maid, and the stranger, may be refreshed.

—Exodus 23:12

Rely on the Sufficiency of Christ

The LORD is my shepherd; I shall not want.

He maketh me to lie down in green pastures: he leadeth me beside the still waters.

He restoreth my soul: he leadeth me in the paths of righteousness for his name's sake.

Yea, though I walk through the valley of the shadow of death, I will fear no evil: for thou art with me; thy rod and thy staff they comfort me.

—Psalm 23:1–4

Such trust have we through Christ to Godward:

Not that we are sufficient of ourselves to think any thing as of ourselves; but our sufficiency is of God.

—2 Corinthians 3:4–5

My help cometh from the LORD, which made heaven and earth.

He will not suffer thy foot to be moved: he that keepeth thee will not slumber.

—Psalm 121:2–3

Seeing then that we have a great high priest, that is passed into the heavens, Jesus the Son of God, let us hold fast our profession.

For we have not an high priest which cannot be touched with the feeling of our infirmities; but was in all points tempted like as we are, yet without sin.

Let us therefore come boldly unto the throne of grace, that we may obtain mercy, and find grace to help in time of need.

—Hebrews 4:14–16

When I saw him, I fell at his feet as dead. And he laid his right hand upon me, saying unto me, Fear not; I am the first and the last:

I am he that liveth, and was dead; and, behold, I am alive for evermore, Amen; and have the keys of hell and of death.

—Revelation 1:17–18

🍃 Find Meaning in Serving the Lord

I said in mine heart concerning the estate of the sons of men, that God might manifest them, and that they might see that they themselves are beasts.

For that which befalleth the sons of men befalleth beasts; even one thing befalleth them: as the one dieth, so dieth the other; yea, they have all one breath; so that a man hath no pre-eminence above a beast: for all is vanity.

All go unto one place; all are of the dust, and all turn to dust again.

—*Ecclesiastes 3:18–20*

Remember now thy Creator in the days of thy youth, while the evil days come not, nor the years draw nigh, when thou shalt say, I have no pleasure in them;

While the sun, or the light, or the moon, or the stars, be not darkened, nor the clouds return after the rain:

In the day when the keepers of the house shall tremble, and the strong men shall bow themselves, and the grinders cease because they are few, and those that look out of the windows be darkened,

And the doors shall be shut in the streets, when the sound of the grinding is low, and he shall rise up at the voice of the bird, and all the daughters of musick shall be brought low;

Also when they shall be afraid of that which is high, and fears shall be in the way, and the almond tree shall flourish, and the grasshopper shall be a burden, and desire shall fail: because man goeth to his long home, and the mourners go about the streets:

Or ever the silver cord be loosed, or the golden bowl be broken, or the pitcher be broken at the fountain, or the wheel broken at the cistern.

Then shall the dust return to the earth as it was: and the spirit shall return unto God who gave it.

—*Ecclesiastes 12:1–7*

How Do I Handle Conflict?

You can be successful in many ways, but if you can't get along with others, you've got a major problem. The Scriptures offer guidance about how to live with our neighbors—the people we love to love . . . and those we'd prefer to hate!

What Will You Do When Conflict Arises?

If I see conflict as natural, neutral, normal, I may be able to see the difficulties we experience as tension in relationships and honest differences in perspective that can be worked through by caring about each other and each confronting the other with truth expressed by love.

—*David Augsburger* [1]

Now I beseech you, brethren, by the name of our Lord Jesus Christ, that ye all speak the same thing, and that there be no divisions among you; but that ye be perfectly joined together in the same mind and in the same judgment.

—*1 Corinthians 1:10*

Lot also, which went with Abram, had flocks, and herds, and tents.

And the land was not able to bear them, that they might dwell together: for their substance was great, so that they could not dwell together.

And there was a strife between the herdmen of Abram's cattle and the herdmen of Lot's cattle: and the Canaanite and the Perizzite dwelled then in the land.

And Abram said unto Lot, Let there be no strife, I pray thee, between me and thee, and between my herdmen and thy herdmen; for we be brethren.

Is not the whole land before thee? separate thyself, I pray thee, from me: if thou wilt take the left hand, then I will go to the right; or if thou depart to the right hand, then I will go to the left.

And Lot lifted up his eyes, and beheld all the plain of Jordan, that it was well watered every where, before the LORD destroyed Sodom and Gomorrah, even as the garden of the LORD, like the land of Egypt, as thou comest unto Zoar.

Then Lot chose him all the plain of Jordan; and Lot journeyed east: and they separated themselves the one from the other.

Abram dwelled in the land of Canaan, and Lot dwelled in the cities of the plain, and pitched his tent toward Sodom.

—Genesis 13:5–12

Then the king went on to Gilgal, and Chimham went on with him: and all the people of Judah conducted the king, and also half the people of Israel.

And, behold, all the men of Israel came to the king, and said unto the king, Why have our brethren the men of Judah stolen thee away, and have brought the king, and his household, and all David's men with him, over Jordan?

And all the men of Judah answered the men of Israel, Because the king is near of kin to us: wherefore then be ye angry for this matter? have we eaten at all of the king's cost? or hath he given us any gift?

And the men of Israel answered the men of Judah, and said, We have ten parts in the king, and we have also more right in David than ye: why then did ye despise us, that our advice should not be first had in bringing back our king? And the words of the men of Judah were fiercer than the words of the men of Israel.

—2 Samuel 19:40–43

Think not that I am come to send peace on earth: I came not to send peace, but a sword.

For I am come to set a man at variance against his father, and the daughter against her mother, and the daughter in law against her mother in law.

And a man's foes shall be they of his own household.

He that loveth father or mother more than me is not worthy of me: and he that loveth son or daughter more than me is not worthy of me.

And he that taketh not his cross, and followeth after me, is not worthy of me.

He that findeth his life shall lose it: and he that loseth his life for my sake shall find it.

—*Matthew 10:34–39*

Again, think ye that we excuse ourselves unto you? we speak before God in Christ: but we do all things, dearly beloved, for your edifying.

For I fear, lest, when I come, I shall not find you such as I would, and that I shall be found unto you such as ye would not: lest there be debates, envyings, wraths, strifes, backbitings, whisperings, swellings, tumults.

—*2 Corinthians 12:19–20*

This is the third time I am coming to you. In the mouth of two or three witnesses shall every word be established.

I told you before, and foretell you, as if I were present, the second time; and being absent now I write to them which heretofore have sinned, and to all other, that, if I come again, I will not spare:

Since ye seek a proof of Christ speaking in me, which to you-ward is not weak, but is mighty in you.

For though he was crucified through weakness, yet he liveth by the power of God. For we also are weak in him, but we shall live with him by the power of God toward you.

Examine yourselves, whether ye be in the faith; prove your own selves. Know ye not your own selves, how that Jesus Christ is in you, except ye be reprobates?

But I trust that ye shall know that we are not reprobates.

Now I pray to God that ye do no evil; not that we should appear approved, but that ye should do that which is honest, though we be as reprobates.

For we can do nothing against the truth,
but for the truth.

For we are glad, when we are weak, and
ye are strong: and this also we wish, even your
perfection.

Therefore I write these things being absent,
lest being present I should use sharpness,
according to the power which the Lord hath
given me to edification, and not to destruction.

—*2 Corinthians 13:1–10*

Finally, be ye all of one mind, having compassion one of another, love as brethren, be
pitiful, be courteous.

—*1 Peter 3:8*

When You're Frustrated . . .

When Peter was come to Antioch, I with-
stood him to the face, because he was to
be blamed.

For before that certain came from James, he
did eat with the Gentiles: but when they were
come, he withdrew and separated himself,
fearing them which were of the circumcision.

And the other Jews dissembled likewise with him; insomuch that Barnabas also was carried away with their dissimulation.

But when I saw that they walked not uprightly according to the truth of the gospel, I said unto Peter before them all, If thou, being a Jew, livest after the manner of Gentiles, and not as do the Jews, why compellest thou the Gentiles to live as do the Jews?

We who are Jews by nature, and not sinners of the Gentiles,

Knowing that a man is not justified by the works of the law, but by the faith of Jesus Christ, even we have believed in Jesus Christ, that we might be justified by the faith of Christ, and not by the works of the law: for by the works of the law shall no flesh be justified.

—*Galatians 2:11–16*

My soul is weary of my life; I will leave my complaint upon myself; I will speak in the bitterness of my soul.

I will say unto God, Do not condemn me; shew me wherefore thou contendest with me.

Is it good unto thee that thou shouldest oppress, that thou shouldest despise the work of thine hands, and shine upon the counsel of the wicked?

Hast thou eyes of flesh? or seest thou as man seeth?

Are thy days as the days of man? are thy years as man's days,

That thou enquirest after mine iniquity, and searchest after my sin?

Thou knowest that I am not wicked; and there is none that can deliver out of thine hand.

Thine hands have made me and fashioned me together round about; yet thou dost destroy me.

Remember, I beseech thee, that thou hast made me as the clay; and wilt thou bring me into dust again?

—Job 10:1–9

I will lift up mine eyes unto the hills, from whence cometh my help.

My help cometh from the LORD, which made heaven and earth.

He will not suffer thy foot to be moved: he that keepeth thee will not slumber.

Behold, he that keepeth Israel shall neither slumber nor sleep.

The LORD is thy keeper: the LORD is thy shade upon thy right hand.

The sun shall not smite thee by day, nor the moon by night.

The LORD shall preserve thee from all evil: he shall preserve thy soul.

The LORD shall preserve thy going out and thy coming in from this time forth, and even for evermore.

—*Psalm 121*

When You're Angry. . .

Some days after Paul said unto Barnabas, Let us go again and visit our brethren in every city where we have preached the word of the Lord, and see how they do.

And Barnabas determined to take with them John, whose surname was Mark.

But Paul thought not good to take him with them, who departed from them from Pamphylia, and went not with them to the work.

And the contention was so sharp between them, that they departed asunder one from the other: and so Barnabas took Mark, and sailed unto Cyprus;

And Paul chose Silas, and departed, being recommended by the brethren unto the grace of God.

And he went through Syria and Cilicia, confirming the churches.

—*Acts 15:36–41*

But I say unto you, That whosoever is angry with his brother without a cause shall be in danger of the judgment: and whosoever shall say to his brother, Raca, shall be in danger of the council: but whosoever shall say, Thou fool, shall be in danger of hell fire.

—*Matthew 5:22*

Be ye angry, and sin not: let not the sun go down upon your wrath:

—*Ephesians 4:26*

🍂 When You Feel Bitter . . .

My soul is weary of my life; I will leave my complaint upon myself; I will speak in the bitterness of my soul.

—*Job 10:1*

Thou hast neither part nor lot in this matter: for thy heart is not right in the sight of God.

Repent therefore of this thy wickedness, and pray God, if perhaps the thought of thine heart may be forgiven thee.

For I perceive that thou art in the gall of bitterness, and in the bond of iniquity.

—*Acts 8:21–23*

Let all bitterness, and wrath, and anger, and clamour, and evil speaking, be put away from you, with all malice.

—*Ephesians 4:31*

Looking diligently lest any man fail of the grace of God; lest any root of bitterness springing up trouble you, and thereby many be defiled.

—*Hebrews 12:15*

Will You Exercise Humility?

It was pride that changed angels into devils; it is humility that makes [us] as angels.

—*Augustine*

I beseech Euodias, and beseech Syntyche, that they be of the same mind in the Lord.

And I intreat thee also, true yokefellow, help those women which laboured with me in the gospel, with Clement also, and with other my fellowlabourers, whose names are in the book of life.

—*Philippians 4:2–3*

Surely he scorneth the scorners: but he giveth grace unto the lowly.

—*Proverbs 3:34*

The fear of the LORD is the instruction of wisdom; and before honour is humility.

—*Proverbs 15:33*

By humility and the fear of the LORD are riches, and honour, and life.

—*Proverbs 22:4*

But I say unto you, That ye resist not evil: but whosoever shall smite thee on thy right cheek, turn to him the other also.

—*Matthew 5:39*

For whosoever exalteth himself shall be abased; and he that humbleth himself shall be exalted.

—*Luke 14:11*

In those days came John the Baptist, preaching in the wilderness of Judaea,

And saying, Repent ye: for the kingdom of heaven is at hand.

For this is he that was spoken of by the prophet Esaias, saying, The voice of one crying in the wilderness, Prepare ye the way of the Lord, make his paths straight.

And the same John had his raiment of camel's hair, and a leathern girdle about his loins; and his meat was locusts and wild honey. . . .

I indeed baptize you with water unto repentance: but he that cometh after me is mightier than I, whose shoes I am not worthy to bear: he shall baptize you with the Holy Ghost, and with fire.

—Matthew 3:1–4, 11

As Jesus passed forth from thence, he saw a man, named Matthew, sitting at the receipt of custom: and he saith unto him, Follow me. And he arose, and followed him.

And it came to pass, as Jesus sat at meat in the house, behold, many publicans and sinners came and sat down with him and his disciples.

And when the Pharisees saw it, they said unto his disciples, Why eateth your Master with publicans and sinners?

But when Jesus heard that, he said unto them, They that be whole need not a physician, but they that are sick.

But go ye and learn what that meaneth, I will have mercy, and not sacrifice: for I am not come to call the righteous, but sinners to repentance.

—Matthew 9:9–13

Whosoever therefore shall confess me before men, him will I confess also before my Father which is in heaven.

But whosoever shall deny me before men, him will I also deny before my Father which is in heaven.

—*Matthew 10:32–33*

Ye adulterers and adulteresses, know ye not that the friendship of the world is enmity with God? whosoever therefore will be a friend of the world is the enemy of God.

Do ye think that the scripture saith in vain, The spirit that dwelleth in us lusteth to envy?

But he giveth more grace. Wherefore he saith, God resisteth the proud, but giveth grace unto the humble.

—*James 4:4–6*

Humble yourselves therefore under the mighty hand of God, that he may exalt you in due time.

—*1 Peter 5:6*

Will You Learn to Be Content?

Whatever comes, let's be content withall:
Among God's blessings there is not one small.
—Robert Herrick

Godliness with contentment is great gain.
For we brought nothing into this world,
and it is certain we can carry nothing out.
And having food and raiment let us be
therewith content.

—*1 Timothy 6:6–8*

[King David] said unto Barzillai, Come
thou over with me, and I will feed thee with
me in Jerusalem.

And Barzillai said unto the king, How long
have I to live, that I should go up with the
king unto Jerusalem?

I am this day fourscore years old: and can I
discern between good and evil? can thy servant
taste what I eat or what I drink? can I hear any
more the voice of singing men and singing
women? wherefore then should thy servant be
yet a burden unto my lord the king?

Thy servant will go a little way over Jordan with the king: and why should the king recompense it me with such a reward?

Let thy servant, I pray thee, turn back again, that I may die in mine own city, and be buried by the grave of my father and of my mother. But behold thy servant Chimham; let him go over with my lord the king; and do to him what shall seem good unto thee.

—*2 Samuel 19:33–37*

For a day in thy courts is better than a thousand. I had rather be a doorkeeper in the house of my God, than to dwell in the tents of wickedness.

For the LORD God is a sun and shield: the LORD will give grace and glory: no good thing will he withhold from them that walk uprightly.

O LORD of hosts, blessed is the man that trusteth in thee.

—*Psalm 84:10–12*

Two things have I required of thee; deny me them not before I die:

Remove far from me vanity and lies: give me neither poverty nor riches; feed me with food convenient for me:

Lest I be full, and deny thee, and say, Who is the LORD? or lest I be poor, and steal, and take the name of my God in vain.

—*Proverbs 30:7–9*

I know that there is no good in them, but for a man to rejoice, and to do good in his life.

And also that every man should eat and drink, and enjoy the good of all his labour, it is the gift of God.

—*Ecclesiastes 3:12–13*

Behold that which I have seen: it is good and comely for one to eat and to drink, and to enjoy the good of all his labour that he taketh under the sun all the days of his life, which God giveth him: for it is his portion.

Every man also to whom God hath given riches and wealth, and hath given him power to eat thereof, and to take his portion, and to rejoice in his labour; this is the gift of God.

For he shall not much remember the days of his life; because God answereth him in the joy of his heart.

—*Ecclesiastes 5:18–20*

All the labour of man is for his mouth, and yet the appetite is not filled.

For what hath the wise more than the fool? what hath the poor, that knoweth to walk before the living?

Better is the sight of the eyes than the wandering of the desire: this is also vanity and vexation of spirit.

—*Ecclesiastes 6:7–9*

Not that I speak in respect of want: for I have learned, in whatsoever state I am, therewith to be content.

I know both how to be abased, and I know how to abound: every where and in all things I am instructed both to be full and to be hungry, both to abound and to suffer need.

I can do all things through Christ which strengtheneth me.

—*Philippians 4:11–13*

Let your conversation be without covetousness; and be content with such things as ye have: for he hath said, I will never leave thee, nor forsake thee.

—Hebrews 13:5

Will You Let God's Peace Comfort You?

Resign every forbidden joy; restrain every wish that is not referred to God's will; banish all eager desires, all anxiety. Desire only the will of God; seek him alone and supremely, and you will find peace.

—Francois Fenelon

Thou shalt make thy prayer unto him, and he shall hear thee, and thou shalt pay thy vows.

Thou shalt also decree a thing, and it shall be established unto thee: and the light shall shine upon thy ways.

When men are cast down, then thou shalt say, There is lifting up; and he shall save the humble person.

He shall deliver the island of the innocent: and it is delivered by the pureness of thine hands.

—*Job 22:27–30*

Dominion and fear are with him, he maketh peace in his high places.

Is there any number of his armies? and upon whom doth not his light arise?

How then can man be justified with God? or how can he be clean that is born of a woman?

Behold even to the moon, and it shineth not; yea, the stars are not pure in his sight.

How much less man, that is a worm? and the son of man, which is a worm?

—*Job 25:2–6*

What man is he that feareth the LORD? him shall he teach in the way that he shall choose.

His soul shall dwell at ease; and his seed shall inherit the earth.

—*Psalm 25:12–13*

The wolf also shall dwell with the lamb, and the leopard shall lie down with the kid; and the calf and the young lion and the fatling together; and a little child shall lead them.

And the cow and the bear shall feed; their young ones shall lie down together: and the lion shall eat straw like the ox.

And the sucking child shall play on the hole of the asp, and the weaned child shall put his hand on the cockatrice' den.

They shall not hurt nor destroy in all my holy mountain: for the earth shall be full of the knowledge of the LORD, as the waters cover the sea.

And in that day there shall be a root of Jesse, which shall stand for an ensign of the people; to it shall the Gentiles seek: and his rest shall be glorious.

And it shall come to pass in that day, that the Lord shall set his hand again the second time to recover the remnant of his people, which shall be left, from Assyria, and from Egypt, and from Pathros, and from Cush, and from Elam, and from Shinar, and from Hamath, and from the islands of the sea.

And he shall set up an ensign for the nations, and shall assemble the outcasts of Israel, and gather together the dispersed of Judah from the four corners of the earth.

The envy also of Ephraim shall depart, and the adversaries of Judah shall be cut off: Ephraim shall not envy Judah, and Judah shall not vex Ephraim.

—Isaiah 11:6–13

[The Lord] will destroy in this mountain the face of the covering cast over all people, and the veil that is spread over all nations.

He will swallow up death in victory; and the Lord GOD will wipe away tears from off all faces; and the rebuke of his people shall he take away from off all the earth: for the LORD hath spoken it.

—Isaiah 25:7–8

Now the God of hope fill you with all joy and peace in believing, that ye may abound in hope, through the power of the Holy Ghost. . . .

Now the God of peace be with you all.
Amen.

—Romans 15:13, 33

And the peace of God, which passeth all understanding, shall keep your hearts and minds through Christ Jesus.

Finally, brethren, whatsoever things are true, whatsoever things are honest, whatsoever things are just, whatsoever things are pure, whatsoever things are lovely, whatsoever things are of good report; if there be any virtue, and if there be any praise, think on these things.

Those things, which ye have both learned, and received, and heard, and seen in me, do: and the God of peace shall be with you.

—Philippians 4:7–9

Can I Be Thankful Every Day?

Someone has said that the most significant thing we can teach our children is the habit of gratitude. Would you agree? Have you learned that lesson yet? After all, every good thing that comes into our lives is a gift from God. How can we help but lift our hearts in praise every day?

Just Consider God's Blessings!

Good when He gives, supremely good,
Nor less when He denies.
E'en crosses from His sovereign hand
Are blessings in disguise.

—Old Hymn

Blessed be the God and Father of our Lord Jesus Christ, who hath blessed us with all spiritual blessings in heavenly places in Christ:

According as he hath chosen us in him before the foundation of the world, that we should be holy and without blame before him in love:

Having predestinated us unto the adoption of children by Jesus Christ to himself, according to the good pleasure of his will,

To the praise of the glory of his grace, wherein he hath made us accepted in the beloved.

In whom we have redemption through his blood, the forgiveness of sins, according to the riches of his grace;

Wherein he hath abounded toward us in all wisdom and prudence;

Having made known unto us the mystery of his will, according to his good pleasure which he hath purposed in himself:

That in the dispensation of the fulness of times he might gather together in one all things in Christ, both which are in heaven, and which are on earth; even in him:

In whom also we have obtained an inheritance, being predestinated according to the purpose of him who worketh all things after the counsel of his own will:

That we should be to the praise of his glory, who first trusted in Christ.

In whom ye also trusted, after that ye heard the word of truth, the gospel of your salvation: in whom also after that ye believed, ye were sealed with that holy Spirit of promise,

Which is the earnest of our inheritance until the redemption of the purchased possession, unto the praise of his glory.

—*Ephesians 1:3–14*

Strengthened with all might, according to his glorious power, unto all patience and longsuffering with joyfulness;

Giving thanks unto the Father, which hath made us meet to be partakers of the inheritance of the saints in light.

—*Colossians 1:11–12*

Every good gift and every perfect gift is from above, and cometh down from the Father of lights, with whom is no variableness, neither shadow of turning.

Of his own will begat he us with the word of truth, that we should be a kind of firstfruits of his creatures.

—*James 1:17–18*

Praise Him for His Saving Promises . . .

"But what can mortal man do to secure his own salvation?" We can do just what God bids us do. We can repent and believe. We can arise and follow Christ as Matthew did.

—*Washington Gladden*

As Jesus passed forth from thence, he saw a man, named Matthew, sitting at the receipt of custom: and he saith unto him, Follow me. And he arose, and followed him.

—*Matthew 9:9*

For mine eyes have seen thy salvation.
Which thou hast prepared before the face of all people.

—*Luke 2:30–31*

🍃 *Of Atonement*

For it pleased the Father that in him should all fulness dwell;
And, having made peace through the blood of his cross, by him to reconcile all things unto himself; by him, I say, whether they be things in earth, or things in heaven.

—*Colossians 1:19–20*

By the which will we are sanctified through the offering of the body of Jesus Christ once for all.
And every priest standeth daily ministering and offering oftentimes the same sacrifices, which can never take away sins

But this man, after he had offered one sacrifice for sins for ever, sat down on the right hand of God;

From henceforth expecting till his enemies be made his footstool.

For by one offering he hath perfected for ever them that are sanctified.

—Hebrews 10:10–14

Of Forgiveness

My little children, these things write I unto you, that ye sin not. And if any man sin, we have an advocate with the Father, Jesus Christ the righteous:

And he is the propitiation for our sins: and not for ours only, but also for the sins of the whole world. . . .

I write unto you, little children, because your sins are forgiven you for his name's sake.

—1 John 2:1–2, 12

But if we walk in the light, as he is in the light, we have fellowship one with another, and the blood of Jesus Christ his Son cleanseth us from all sin.

If we say that we have no sin, we deceive ourselves, and the truth is not in us.

If we confess our sins, he is faithful and just to forgive us our sins, and to cleanse us from all unrighteousness.

—1 John 1:7–9

For I will be merciful to their unrighteousness, and their sins and their iniquities will I remember no more.

—Hebrews 8:12

Of Redemption from Sin

The Son of man came not to be ministered unto, but to minister, and to give his life a ransom for many.

—Matthew 20:28

Being justified freely by his grace through the redemption that is in Christ Jesus:

Whom God hath set forth to be a propitiation through faith in his blood, to declare his righteousness for the remission of sins that are past, through the forbearance of God;

To declare, I say, at this time his righteousness: that he might be just, and the justifier of him which believeth in Jesus.

—Romans 3:24–26

But of him are ye in Christ Jesus, who of God is made unto us wisdom, and righteousness, and sanctification, and redemption.

—1 Corinthians 1:30

For ye are bought with a price: therefore glorify God in your body, and in your spirit, which are God's.

—1 Corinthians 6:20

I am crucified with Christ: nevertheless I live; yet not I, but Christ liveth in me: and the life which I now live in the flesh I live by the faith of the Son of God, who loved me, and gave himself for me.

—Galatians 2:20

Of New Birth

Verily, verily, I say unto thee, Except a man be born again, he cannot see the kingdom of God.

Nicodemus saith unto him, How can a man be born when he is old? can he enter the second time into his mother's womb, and be born?

Jesus answered, Verily, verily, I say unto thee, Except a man be born of water and of the Spirit, he cannot enter into the kingdom of God.

That which is born of the flesh is flesh; and that which is born of the Spirit is spirit.

Marvel not that I said unto thee, Ye must be born again.

The wind bloweth where it listeth, and thou hearest the sound thereof, but canst not tell whence it cometh, and whither it goeth: so is every one that is born of the Spirit.

—*John 3:3–8*

In whom also ye are circumcised with the circumcision made without hands, in putting off the body of the sins of the flesh by the circumcision of Christ:

Buried with him in baptism, wherein also ye are risen with him through the faith of the operation of God, who hath raised him from the dead.

And you, being dead in your sins and the uncircumcision of your flesh, hath he quickened together with him, having forgiven you all trespasses.

—*Colossians 2:11–13*

Elect according to the foreknowledge of God the Father, through sanctification of the Spirit, unto obedience and sprinkling of the blood of Jesus Christ: Grace unto you, and peace, be multiplied.

Blessed be the God and Father of our Lord Jesus Christ, which according to his abundant mercy hath begotten us again unto a lively hope by the resurrection of Jesus Christ from the dead.

—*1 Peter 1:2–3*

Seeing ye have purified your souls in obeying the truth through the Spirit unto unfeigned love of the brethren, see that ye love one another with a pure heart fervently

Being born again, not of corruptible seed,
but of incorruptible, by the word of God,
which liveth and abideth for ever.

—*1 Peter 1:22–23*

Of Adoption as God's Children

For as many as are led by the Spirit of God,
they are the sons of God.

For ye have not received the spirit of bondage again to fear; but ye have received the
Spirit of adoption, whereby we cry, Abba,
Father.

The Spirit itself beareth witness with our
spirit, that we are the children of God:

And if children, then heirs; heirs of God,
and joint-heirs with Christ; if so be that we
suffer with him, that we may be also glorified
together.

For I reckon that the sufferings of this
present time are not worthy to be compared
with the glory which shall be revealed in us.

For the earnest expectation of the creature
waiteth for the manifestation of the sons
of God.

For the creature was made subject to vanity, not willingly, but by reason of him who hath subjected the same in hope,

Because the creature itself also shall be delivered from the bondage of corruption into the glorious liberty of the children of God. . . .

For whom he did foreknow, he also did predestinate to be conformed to the image of his Son, that he might be the firstborn among many brethren.

—*Romans 8:14–21, 29*

For it became him, for whom are all things, and by whom are all things, in bringing many sons unto glory, to make the captain of their salvation perfect through sufferings.

For both he that sanctifieth and they who are sanctified are all of one: for which cause he is not ashamed to call them brethren,

Saying, I will declare thy name unto my brethren, in the midst of the church will I sing praise unto thee.

And again, I will put my trust in him. And again, Behold I and the children which God hath given me.

—*Hebrews 2:10–13*

🍃 *Of Sanctification*

Sanctify them through thy truth: thy word is truth.

As thou hast sent me into the world, even so have I also sent them into the world.

And for their sakes I sanctify myself, that they also might be sanctified through the truth.

—*John 17:17–19*

Now he which stablisheth us with you in Christ, and hath anointed us, is God;

Who hath also sealed us, and given the earnest of the Spirit in our hearts.

—*2 Corinthians 1:21–22*

For this is the will of God, even your sanctification, that ye should abstain from fornication:

That every one of you should know how to possess his vessel in sanctification and honour.

—*1 Thessalonians 4:3–4*

But we are bound to give thanks alway to God for you, brethren beloved of the Lord, because God hath from the beginning chosen you to salvation through sanctification of the Spirit and belief of the truth:

Whereunto he called you by our gospel, to the obtaining of the glory of our Lord Jesus Christ.

—2 Thessalonians 2:13–14

Cultivate a Spirit of Gratitude for All Things

Gratitude is born in hearts that take time to count up past mercies.

—Charles Jefferson

In every thing give thanks: for this is the will of God in Christ Jesus concerning you.

—1 Thessalonians 5:18

Be careful for nothing; but in every thing by prayer and supplication with thanksgiving let your requests be made known unto God.

—Philippians 4:6

The LORD is the portion of mine inheritance and of my cup: thou maintainest my lot.

The lines are fallen unto me in pleasant places; yea, I have a goodly heritage.

—*Psalm 16:5–6*

Thou hast turned for me my mourning into dancing: thou hast put off my sackcloth, and girded me with gladness;

To the end that my glory may sing praise to thee, and not be silent. O LORD my God, I will give thanks unto thee for ever.

—*Psalm 30:11–12*

He maketh the barren woman to keep house, and to be a joyful mother of children. Praise ye the LORD.

—*Pslam 113:9*

They that sow in tears shall reap in joy.

He that goeth forth and weepeth, bearing precious seed, shall doubtless come again with rejoicing, bringing his sheaves with him.

—*Psalm 126:5–6*

Sing, O ye heavens; for the LORD hath done it: shout, ye lower parts of the earth: break forth into singing, ye mountains, O forest, and every tree therein: for the LORD hath redeemed Jacob, and glorified himself in Israel.

—*Isaiah 44:23*

My brethren, count it all joy when ye fall into divers temptations;

Knowing this, that the trying of your faith worketh patience.

But let patience have her perfect work, that ye may be perfect and entire, wanting nothing.

If any of you lack wisdom, let him ask of God, that giveth to all men liberally, and upbraideth not; and it shall be given him.

But let him ask in faith, nothing wavering. For he that wavereth is like a wave of the sea driven with the wind and tossed.

—*James 1:2–6*

But rejoice, inasmuch as ye are partakers of Christ's sufferings; that, when his glory shall be revealed, ye may be glad also with exceed-ing joy.

—*1 Peter 4:13*

Offer Praise and Thanks Every Day

God, I give You the praise for days well spent. But I am yet unsatisfied, because I do not enjoy enough of You. I apprehend myself at too great a distance from You. I would have my soul more closely united to You by faith and love.

—*Susanna Wesley*

I will sing of the mercies of the LORD for ever: with my mouth will I make known thy faithfulness to all generations.

For I have said, Mercy shall be built up for ever: thy faithfulness shalt thou establish in the very heavens.

I have made a covenant with my chosen, I have sworn unto David my servant,

Thy seed will I establish for ever, and build up thy throne to all generations. Selah.

—*Psalm 89:1–4*

The LORD shall increase you more and more, you and your children.

Ye are blessed of the LORD which made heaven and earth.

The heaven, even the heavens, are the LORD's: but the earth hath he given to the children of men.

The dead praise not the LORD, neither any that go down into silence.

But we will bless the LORD from this time forth and for evermore. Praise the LORD.

—Psalm 115:14–18

I will extol thee, my God, O king; and I will bless thy name for ever and ever.

Every day will I bless thee; and I will praise thy name for ever and ever.

Great is the LORD, and greatly to be praised; and his greatness is unsearchable.

One generation shall praise thy works to another, and shall declare thy mighty acts.

—Psalm 145:1–4

Praise ye the LORD. Praise God in his sanctuary: praise him in the firmament of his power.

Praise him for his mighty acts: praise him according to his excellent greatness.

Praise him with the sound of the trumpet: praise him with the psaltery and harp.

Praise him with the timbrel and dance: praise him with stringed instruments and organs.

Praise him upon the loud cymbals: praise him upon the high sounding cymbals.

Let every thing that hath breath praise the LORD. Praise ye the LORD.

—Psalm 150

The heavens declare the glory of God; and the firmament sheweth his handywork.

Day unto day uttereth speech, and night unto night sheweth knowledge.

There is no speech nor language, where their voice is not heard.

Their line is gone out through all the earth, and their words to the end of the world. In them hath he set a tabernacle for the sun.

—Psalm 19:1–4

The LORD shall increase you more and more, you and your children.

Ye are blessed of the LORD which made heaven and earth.

The heaven, even the heavens, are the LORD's: but the earth hath he given to the children of men.

The dead praise not the LORD, neither any that go down into silence.

But we will bless the LORD from this time forth and for evermore. Praise the LORD.

—*Psalm 115:14–18*

This is the day which the LORD hath made; we will rejoice and be glad in it.

—*Psalm 118:24*

Echo the Psalmist's Worshipful Example

For worship is a thirsty land crying out for rain,
   It is a candle in the act of being kindled,
      It is a drop in quest of the ocean . . .
   It is a voice in the night calling for help,
It is a soul standing in awe before the mystery of
      the universe . . .
      It is time flowing into eternity . . .
   a man climbing the altar stairs to God.

—*Dwight Bradley [1]*

Praise ye the LORD. Praise ye the name of the LORD; praise him, O ye servants of the LORD.

Ye that stand in the house of the LORD, in the courts of the house of our God,

Praise the LORD; for the LORD is good: sing praises unto his name; for it is pleasant.

For the LORD hath chosen Jacob unto himself, and Israel for his peculiar treasure.

For I know that the LORD is great, and that our Lord is above all gods.

Whatsoever the LORD pleased, that did he in heaven, and in earth, in the seas, and all deep places.

He causeth the vapours to ascend from the ends of the earth; he maketh lightnings for the rain; he bringeth the wind out of his treasuries.

Who smote the firstborn of Egypt, both of man and beast.

Who sent tokens and wonders into the midst of thee, O Egypt, upon Pharaoh, and upon all his servants.

Who smote great nations, and slew mighty kings;

Sihon king of the Amorites, and Og king of Bashan, and all the kingdoms of Canaan:

And gave their land for an heritage, an heritage unto Israel his people.

Thy name, O LORD, endureth for ever; and thy memorial, O LORD, throughout all generations.

For the LORD will judge his people, and he will repent himself concerning his servants.

The idols of the heathen are silver and gold, the work of men's hands.

They have mouths, but they speak not; eyes have they, but they see not;

They have ears, but they hear not; neither is there any breath in their mouths.

They that make them are like unto them: so is every one that trusteth in them.

Bless the LORD, O house of Israel: bless the LORD, O house of Aaron:

Bless the LORD, O house of Levi: ye that fear the LORD, bless the LORD.

Blessed be the LORD out of Zion, which dwelleth at Jerusalem. Praise ye the LORD.

—Psalm 135

$\mathcal{N}$otes

—Chapter Two—

1 Frederick Buechner, *The Magnificent Defeat.*
2 A statement from the *Talmud.*
3 Gerald May, in *The Shalem Newsletter,* vol. 18, #1.

—Chapter Four—

1 R.G. Lee, *Pickings.*
2 Source unknown.
3 Frederick Buechner, *Wishful Thinking* (San Francisco: HarperSanFrancisco, 1993).

—Chapter Five—

1 Phillip Yancey, *Unhappy Secrets of the Christian Life* (Grand Rapids: Zondervan, and Wheaton, Ill.: Campus Life Books, 1979).
2 Dietrich Bonhoeffer, *The Cost of Discipleship* (New York: Macmillan, 1961).
3 Leo Tolstoy, in a letter to his son.

—Chapter Six—

1 Alexander Solzhenitsyn, *The First Circle,* trans. Thomas P. Whitney (New York and Evanston: Harper & Row, 1968).

—Chapter Seven—

1 Walter Trobisch, in *Men's Devotional Bible* (Grand Rapids: Zondervan, 1993).

—Chapter Eight—

1 David Augsburger, *Caring Enough to Confront* (Glendale, Calif.: GL / Regal Books, 1976).

—Chapter Nine—

1 Dwight Bradley, in *Leaves from a Spiritual Notebook*, as quoted in Frank S. Mead, ed., *12,000 Religious Quotations* (Grand Rapids: Baker, 1992).